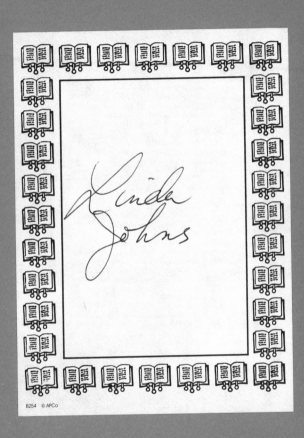

Linda Johns

8254 © APCo

Sharing a Robin's Life

LINDA JOHNS

NIMBUS
PUBLISHING

Tribute
acrylic on paper, 1991

FOR COUNTY,
and all those who helped me to contribute to her happiness.

Nimbus Publishing Limited
P.O. Box 9301, Station A
Halifax, N.S.
B3K 5N5
(902) 455-4286

Design: GDA, Halifax
Printed and bound in Hong Kong

Canadian Cataloguing in Publication Data
Johns, Linda.
Sharing a robin's life
ISBN 1-55109-004-X (Bound)—1-55109-055-4 (Pbk.)
1. Robin as pets. I. Title.
SF473.T48J64 1992 C818.5403 C92-098511-4

AUTHOR'S NOTES
These chronicles of the interwoven years of a robin and a human have been set down to provide insights into one songbird's existence, from nestlinghood to maturity and motherhood. In many ways we are all similar in our experiences of happiness, grief, frustration, fear and contentment, as well as in our dependency upon the earth's provender for ourselves and our offspring. As human guardians of this planet, our concern must not terminate when our own personal needs are fulfilled. Instead, our scope must be enlarged to include, without question, the needs of even the least of creatures sharing our world—for the benefit of all.

Perhaps we ought to take another look at the Native American cultures that guide today's decisions by their concern for the well-being of the seventh generation yet to come.

It is my hope that sharing County's teachings in this book can contribute to this wider vision.

LINDA JOHNS

INTRODUCTION

THIS IS A TRUE STORY of two unusual individuals. It revolves around a robin that was old enough, when found, to have escaped the "imprinting" process used by researchers such as Konrad Lorenz to gain a bird's trust and confidence. Imprinting occurs shortly after most young birds hatch, when they identify with the individual who takes care of them. Normally, parents are involved. When humans displace them, young birds accept the substitute parent. In this way Greylag geese and other species can live out their lives accepting humans as part of the family. Some birds will even reject their own species as mates, accepting a human mate instead. This sounds like a terrible distortion, but it permits peregrine falcon researchers, for example, to collect semen for artificial insemination. In this way, people can help an endangered species to regain its population.

County, the robin in this story, had no such illusions about her identity. So, why didn't she leave when given the chance?

The answer had something to do with the robin's personality, but also with the extraordinary nature of the human in this story, Linda Johns. Many people have found and raised young robins. With food and care, they grow and begin to act like they own the place. Eventually, the house becomes too small, and the robin is released.

Linda is an artist who lives in the woods of rural Nova Scotia and values her privacy. She is an intense person who invests tremendous amounts of time and energy to her art. When County arrived, Linda's focus shifted to a bundle of feathers. Her attentiveness and willingness to accommodate County exceeded normal human sensitivities. County responded. A bond was created.

On a recommendation from a friend who knew me as a biologist who rehabilitated injured wildlife and reared wild orphans, Linda telephoned me for help with County's nesting aspirations. At first a scientific consultant, I came to be a friend who witnessed many of the activities that Linda describes in this book.

Textbooks state that only male robins sing the familiar cheeri-ly-cheerily song. County blew that fact, and others, out of the water. This book offers new insights into robin behaviour; activities not documented in previous publications. A number of major studies of robin behaviour and life history have been unable to offer much information about some important aspects of their lives. No one has reported any specific courtship activities before. The only activity witnessed until this study amounted to abrupt copulation. This led some researchers to conclude that no courtship behaviour exists. But how could pair formation occur without some form of display? Linda's observations indicate that courtship is far from a hit and miss affair, and that robins have been secretive about their private lives in previous studies.

Vocalizations have been another enigma for researchers. Linda learned to recognize County's requests for a specific type of food. When babies refuse to open their mouths to be fed, Linda could prompt County to elicit the "open-your-mouth" call for her. This book sheds new light upon robin vocalization.

Often, County's behaviour raised more questions for me than it resolved. For example, how did she adjust her brooding by touching her beak to the baby? Did she use her beak as a ther-mometer, or to sense a heart rate that varied with temperature? Human science has only scratched the surface of wildlife knowl-edge. And robins, one of the few wild birds that most North Americans can identify, are virtually unknown to us. Like blue jays, they keep their privacy, while still living close to humans.

Until recently, science held that man was the only "thinking" or "conscious" animal. This egocentric view was further clouded by the "domination over animals" status conferred upon us by the Bible, but open to interpretation. "Dominion" might imply responsibility for other animals. Noah certainly tried!

David Hume volunteered the philosophical opinion in 1739 that "no truth appears to me to be more evident, than that beasts are endow'd with thought and reason as well as men." Until recently modern science leaned heavily in the opposite direction, attributing animal behaviour only to instinct and genetic programming. Animals such as insects and spiders were observed to accomplish elaborate patterns of behaviour on the first appropriate occasion, without having any chance to learn what needed to be done. This absence of learning was considered proof that animals had no conscious awareness of their instinctive actions.

Recent books such as Animal Thinking, by Donald Griffin, point out flaws in the imaginary "thinking" wall that we have constructed around ourselves. Animals can adjust their behaviour to solve problems. To some scientists, this implies an ability to think and feel consciously. Have humans been too insensitive to understand the emotional depths and complicated lives of many species that share the Earth? Ethology, the comparative study of social behaviour patterns, has helped to place humans in a more realistic context with other animals by raising embarassing facts. Why do some animals utter warning cries to others, when their own lives are threatened by predators in the process? Why would younger bluejays guide an older, partially blind jay to places to bathe and feed? Man's "ivory tower" assumption of being the only animal capable of conscious thought is crumbling.

After reading Linda's book, some readers will accept that robins can think, reason, have emotions, and communicate through vocalizations, "looks," and displays that can actually be learned by other species; even humans. These abilities extend well into the depths of communication that humans have traditionally considered sacred territory. Others will conclude that we are daft; particularly after reading about such unusual incidents as the collective reaction of Linda's feathered houseguests to her operation at the hospital. I can offer no explanation by current science; only the assurance that I know the two people involved, as well as the birds, and that it happened. If humans continue to survive as a species on this planet, it will be in part by learning to live with nature. Should we reach that level, such incidents may someday be more commonplace and scientifically verifiable. We might even develop the kind of awareness, respect and reverence for nature once held by North American Indians.

The photographs in this book are not by professionals in staged settings after the fact. They were taken when events occurred. These photographs are a visual record of what actually happened.

Please do not decide to find a baby robin for your home after reading this book. County occupied a major portion of Linda's life for many years. Few people could make the investment of time, energy and emotion. Anything less would have been inadequate. There is also a legal reason for not taking wildlife out of its natural environment. Most migratory birds are protected by Federal laws that forbid such actions. Other birds are protected by provincial or state legislation. This story falls through the legislative cracks, since County needed help when she was first found, an "authority" (provincial biologist) was notified, and freedom was offered after she recovered.

The efforts devoted to solving the major problems of our "civilization" continue to be neither adequate or sensible. County's wealth of spirit will continue in Linda Johns' paintings, which are powerful testimonies to strong forces struggling in a natural world under siege from indifference and our exploding human population.

BOB BANCROFT

CHAPTER ONE
DISCOVERY

WHEN I FIRST SAW HER, she was an eight-or nine-day-old robin fledgling crouched at the side of the road, and too young to be on her own. Putting her up on the branch of a nearby apple tree, I withdrew and waited to see if one of the parents would appear. Predators, however, have a way of dividing families. An hour later I carried her into the house with the intention of launching her in a couple of weeks; something I'd done numerous times before with other separated youngsters.

Except that she never did leave, and that was a turning point in both our lives.

Her efforts to satisfy her own particular needs within the whirl of a busy human environment led to her rather unusual name. Calling insistently when she was hungry, only to be overlooked, would provoke her finally to hurl herself straight into the core of the prevailing activity, her beak gaping determinedly, and personifying in every indignant feather the rural expression "another county heard from." So County she came to be called.

OUR home is a rambling ground-level building with a loft and high cathedral ceiling at one end. It is beautifully surrounded by acres of woodland and meadows. Trees close to the house bring wild bird activities continually into close range and provide frequent sightings of other wild creatures as well. County was never caged; the entire house was always at her disposal, and the daily unfolding of her life within its precincts was an illumination and a rare privilege.

Within a week of her arrival County developed an insistent chronic cough which persisted for many months before finally ceasing. I decided against her leaving, feeling that she'd never migrate successfully with a breathing handicap. Anyway, by that time she was reigning supreme over the establishment and leaving didn't seem to be on her mind.

I fed her a variety of foods for which she gaped readily: currants, worms, bugs, fresh fruit, canned dog food, cheese, lean ground beef, and cooked egg yolk. I would dip the occasional tidbit in water, shaking off the excess, since she hadn't learned to drink yet. She needed food, in quantities of two or three caterpillars' worth, roughly every half-hour, from dawn to dusk and would call repeatedly when hungry. This call was not to be confused with her steady "location" note between feedings, a sort of radio contact between fledglings and foraging parents to which I tried to respond verbally for reassurance.

Not distinguishing between these two calls has led many well-intentioned people to overfeed stray nestlings. This often results in death. I found that a good way to regulate County's feeding schedule was to put myself in a parent bird's position faced with three or four hungry youngsters. I would imagine myself flying off and hunting patiently through the foliage, returning finally with about two fat caterpillars (a beak-size serving) which would quickly disappear down the throat of nestling number one. Then I'd remove the fecal sac produced invariably at this time, drop it well away from the nest, and go off to find two or three more wrigglies for nestling number two, and so on. By the time I'd get the last one fed, it would be time to feed the first one again— about twenty minutes later. Imagining the process in this way helped to prevent me from overfeeding County.

For the first week County slept on towels in a little draped box in a warm area near a lamp. When she objected to being bedded in it each night so strongly as to bounce up against the cover over and over again like a stubborn little feathered frog, I let her choose her own roosts. Sometimes she'd select the shower curtain rod, the upstairs closet, the back porch, the horn of a wall-hung cowskull, or the drying pegs protruding from a hand-hewn beam in the living room. She always changed the chosen spot every two or three days, leading me to speculate if that were a necessary safety maneuver in the wild, because of scent buildup, or perhaps because of accumulated droppings below (although she did very few at night.)

Gradually County became more and more mobile, ever on the go, bursting with curiosity about everything and endowed with a lively teasing nature. Two frequent victims of her devilishness were Desmond and Molly, a pair of young domestic pigeons who had arrived a couple of months previously when they were about ten days old—winsome but woebegone. Desmond had been battered and defeathered by a flock of grown pigeons and Molly was suffering from an impacted crop. Mild disinfectant and warmth for Des, a mineral-oil tonic and crop massage for Molly, and a softened nourishing diet for both had worked wonders so that by County's arrival they were feathered, flying and bright-eyed. They were never caged either and had more flying room indoors than I could have afforded outdoors with the costs of weasel-proof wire caging. A few shelves on the wall for feed dishes and roosts gave them a secure base from which they pattered about the floors with timid curiosity, always keeping near each other with rounded eyes of wonder. Gradually their confidence grew and they would bask daily in a warm patch of sunlight on the floor, getting up again and again to follow it as it glided through the house. But their innately gentle nature collided frequently with County's exuberant cockiness, setting the stage for endless entertainment. Their idea of quiet amusement was to play with a heap of buttons I'd given them, toying with them, and tossing them up to fall. County's idea of amusement was to snatch the buttons out of their mouths in passing and drop them onto their heads from above. There were moments when she teased them mercilessly—like swooping over Desmond from behind and thumping him on the head with her feet en route. She continually desecrated the clean drinking water in their bowl by bathing in it, dropping buttons—or—worse into it, and periodically indulged in scattering their food pellets and grit over a surprisingly wide range. If they were dozing, nothing delighted her more than swooping them repeatedly into ruffled annoyance and then scampering ahead of them as they bore sedately down on her, cooing irritably in the dignified majestic anger of pigeons.

Her greater speed and maneuverability made her almost invulnerable but her overconfidence was her downfall. Hovering over Molly one day and paddling her feet on her head, County suddenly found herself seized by a leg in an unprecedented turning of tables and shaken thoroughly by an irate Molly, who turned a deaf ear to County's plaintive squeaks of pain and remorse. And on more than one occasion, hearing a disturbance, I'd enter a room just as County was streaking out and see mild Desmond dropping a mouthful of robin feathers with evident satisfaction.

To County, *everything* was to be explored. Through her eyes I began to view the house in an altogether different way. What had appeared to be an aesthetically-pleasing whitened cowskull hanging on the wall, was in reality a pair of perches ideal for preening and napping. Lampshades offered electrically-warmed roosts particularly cozy for drying wet feathers after a bath, and the woodbox was a prolific hunting ground for insects. A mundane broom impassively sweeping the floor was actually for challenging and chasing, and the scattered sweepings a positive triumph.

But not every added dimension was so benign. A tall roomy boot, an open crock of honey, or a half-full coffee mug were innocent preludes to disaster for a curious, inexperienced fledgling. Because young robins examine everything by jabbing with their beaks, I became one of the tidiest, if not one of the most paranoid, of mortals, perpetually unplugging appliances and hiding knives and scissors, often to my own personal inconvenience. Moths weren't the only creatures to be attracted to the open flames of candles, and the electric stove at mealtimes contained such a wealth of nightmarish possibilities that I doubted if I'd ever be free of the burden of owning one. Even a sink full of soaking dishes and sharp utensils would loom menacingly with hazards. Spilled spices had to be cornered instantly, and hot baked goods locked in the bathroom to cool, it being the only room with a door—and without mice. Dangling mobiles had to be removed from high-speed flyways, and I developed an intense fixation about pins, thumbtacks, and staples on floors which I found myself indulging even in other peoples' houses. The consequences of neglecting even a stray elastic band was brought suddenly to my attention one morning when County, after playfully toying with one as though it were a worm, swallowed it. Fortunately it caught around her lower mandible and I was able to snatch her up and gently pull the remainder out of her throat in spite of her indignant struggles.

The horrendous possibilities involving thread she thoroughly explored one day when I was out. When I arrived home, the living room looked as though it had been systematically gift-wrapped by a gigantic spider. There was thread joining every visible object. County had discovered an antique spoolholder holding several spools which allowed threads to be pulled out easily. One thing had led to another and, getting several entangled around her feet, she'd flown all over the house and even up into the loft attempting to free herself, while the unwinding threads behind her wrapped themselves liberally around every projection she passed. She'd finally managed to tie herself quite tightly to a large piece of driftwood and was still struggling and terrified when I came in. It was a lesson on thread neither of us ever forgot.

County's enjoyment enriched even the most minute and common occurrences. It became so infectious that I found myself quite sharing her delight as she chased drops of water falling from freshly misted plants or soared astoundingly straight up to the peak of the cathedral ceiling to return triumphantly grasping a tiny spider in her beak—or better yet, one of those shudderingly huge ones that I visualized dropping down on my head some night. Or into my tea. Even the sprinkling of rain on the roof moved her to song in rippling warbles and trills, transmitting to me through the sudden beauty of music, unnoticed changes in the weather outside. The gentle rise and fall of a robin's rain song harmonizes so exquisitely with the fluctuations of pattering raindrops that they will always remain interwoven melodies in my mind.

Even the daily arrival of morning County saluted with jubilant songs and flights more truly worthy of the 'renewal of light' than our usual reception of 'just another day.' She'd start with high-speed flights and loud 'barking' while swooping back and forth through the house at gray dawn, and then land on my head to waken me, pulling my hair and eyelashes impatiently and resorting, when all else failed, to thrusting her bill right down into my ear. This *never* failed. Then she'd flit from windowsill to windowsill, wing-flicking and tail-flicking with bursts of singing, glorying in sun or rain and taking in the bustling activities of the outdoor birds as though seeing it all for the first time—an enviable freshness of mind she retained year after year. And her enthusiasm was decidedly contagious. Once I'd finally been roused, I'd often stand beside her trying (usually in vain) to see just what *she* was seeing—what was provoking that excited bark and terse cocked head with every feather upright in participation? But if after all that time I was still somnolent in a tumble of blankets, County would often nestle down on my head, or nose, or chin—whatever was available—and preen companionably or sing softly.

Even her silence spoke. One still afternoon poised reluctantly on the brink of winter, when only a few scattered yellow leaves were lingering on the trees, and the infinite mingling of summer birdsongs had dwindled to the winter feeder calls of jays, juncos, and grosbeaks, I suddenly missed County. A short search revealed her sitting silently on a windowsill looking out on the late golden light. Sensing the fullness of feeling permeating and surrounding her, I knelt quietly down beside her as she gazed out unblinkingly into the sky.

With eyes huge and dark and far-seeing, she turned her head and, as in a vision, I saw in her eye centuries of migrations crossing the vastness of her inner skies from the eternal springs of memory.

Flights crisscrossing in unending streams, lives upon lives evolving through the ages and all encompassed in the eye of a single bird, an eloquent Eye that loomed as large momentarily as the universe itself...

WITH County, even common household tasks became Events. When I sat down with huge bowls of fresh chanterelle mushrooms resigned to a couple of hours shredding and debugging, she perched on the bowl rim delighting in any bugs I found and often carrying off pieces of mushroom to pound smaller and eat. When I baked, she was usually feet-first into the mixing bowl sampling the batter and extracting raisins, her special favourites. She would stalk impatiently up and down the counter while muffins, another favourite, were baking, peering through the glass door of the oven at them. Frequently I baked just for the fun of doing it with her. If I washed my hands under the kitchen tap, she'd edge down my arm into my cupped hands to enjoy her own shower under the dribble, drenching me to the waist with spray. And her 'raised eyebrows' look from atop the shower curtain rod could convulse me with laughter while I showered.

But proper bathing for County was not just a hasty cleansing process fitted into the most convenient time of day as it has become for most of us. The moment was *selected*—which in itself I found worthy of consideration. And there was a particular ritual to be followed that enhanced and prolonged the intense enjoyment birds always have for bathing. Fresh water, of course, was essential. Stepping into her water dish, stepping out again and fixing me with her eye immediately galvanized me into bringing fresh water. Then she'd hop about in the dish doing speculative beak flicks to test depth, shooting water out in all directions. Choosing the deepest area (due to the tilting dish) she'd indulge in a few tentative wing flicks, gradually accelerate to a watery blur and then suddenly stop, hop out, and coyly feign a brief interest in probing under the dish. Hopping back in, she'd do one or two more wingflicks before really churning up a turmoil of spray by vibrating each wing alternately, as an ever-advancing tidal ring glistened around the dish. At this point, she usually hopped out for a few shakes before returning for more splashing, interrupted by several moments of perfect stillness when she remained motionless with all her feathers puffed out, emitting a tiny high-pitched whistle while the water lapped gently around her. Finally, with another resounding flurry, thoroughly saturated and satisfied, she'd fly heavily to a warm roost to preen, pulling the feathers dry through her beak. Then she'd oil her feathers by taking oil from a special preening gland at the base of her tail and distributing it all over her feet and feathers. The final result was a beautifully-groomed appearance and a prodigious appetite, the satisfaction of which was invariably followed by a prolonged nap. One of her favourite drying roosts was on the gentle curve of an overturned deer antler which was strategically placed under a feather-warming hanging lamp. For me, the shedding process inherent in a cast-off horn is a reminder in the wider sense of the progressive sheddings marking our inner growth. This image was movingly emphasized by the artless charm of this young fledgling, poised awkwardly between nestlinghood and adulthood, and edged in light descending from above.

CHAPTER TWO

UNFOLDING

As OUR COMPANIONSHIP DEVELOPED, I gradually learned from County a robin code of affectionate interaction which was totally different from that of mammals. She was absolutely *not* to be cuddled, patted or picked up bodily. Nor was I to extend a finger-perch to her in order to carry her off with me to another part of the house for company's sake. These gestures, however expressive of fondness were not only unacceptable, but disturbing impositions to her. But frequently, especially if I were overtired or headachy, she would come and nestle down on my forehead as I lay back in my chair, and by the very stillness of her small presence, ease my weariness with a penetrating calm effective enough to banish any indisposition. And she has passed many hours sitting quietly on my shoulder while I read, or on the side of my head, preening and dozing, while I lay in bed in the morning. Joining me for meals and taking tidbits off my tongue, riding on my shoulder, nestling on my chest when I napped, and skimming the top of my head in passing, were all acceptable forms of physical contact.

As for me, the honour and delight of a creature's *choosing* to be near me of its own accord became so preferable that I tended more and more to a passive yet welcoming attitude with nearly all creatures. I even began to feel mildly uncomfortable, perhaps unreasonably so, at someone else's boisterous greetings being imposed on creatures whose natural inclinations would be to express themselves far less demonstratively, albeit just as deeply.

Eye contact between County and I was very important too, as it is among the birds I watch outside who all use vocal interactions to a lesser extent. Reassurance, anxiety, affection, concern, fear—any number of emotions were all expressed between us by eye, which was especially handy, yet subtle, across a room during the sudden appearance of human visitors, an event she seldom failed to find disquieting. Then, a very slow blink of my eyes would convey stabilizing calmness to her. She expressed total trust quite simply by turning her back to me at close range, an honour I've also experienced with a few of my winter feeder regulars, notably wild red squirrels who will sit only two or three feet away with their backs turned, eating spruce cones. County also signified hunger by tugging persistently at my hair, no matter what I was doing, until I finally complied with a tasty snack from the fridge. How she came by that peculiar method (unless it's suggestive of tugging earthworms from the ground for food) and how she transmitted its meaning to me remained a mystery, but it never failed her.

BEGINNING in late summer and continuing through the fall of that first year, County's juvenile plumage of a dark-spotted breast, a light-spotted back and gray under-tail coverts gradually gave way to her adult plumage, enabling me to ascertain her gender—female robins having a lighter colouring overall than males. For some time, her breast was a confusion of dark spots jostling white-edged russet feathers until finally the russet prevailed entirely and her undertail coverts became patterned with white and gray. Her head feathers were the last to moult; for one unforgettable period she presented the amusing combination of a sleek adult robin body crowned with a bald head bristling with highly-unbecoming gray spikes of unopened feathers—reminiscent of a horned toad was my kindest comparison. By the turn of the year, she was beautifully uniform with the added touch of white wing-bars which I've seen only once on another robin. She also had unusually full white eye-rings, was somewhat smaller than most robins, and had slightly shorter wings and tail.

It may be, too, that she had a greater share of cheekiness than most robins, or perhaps her personal environment was more conducive to its development than rigorous outdoor life, but the dust rarely settled in County's immediate vicinity. On one memorable occasion, I was sharing lunch with County and a human friend. Although I had finished eating, County had not, and was avidly

As a youngster, County radiated a lively curiosity about everything (right).

County swoops at Desmond, teasing him mercilessly, while Molly looks on (below).

County loved extracting raisins from fresh-baked muffins (top).

*She also enjoyed saturating her plumage in quick showers
under the tap (above right and left).*

During moulting time, County's head feathers would be the last to change (above); afterward, her full eye-rings and white wingbars were highly distinctive (above right).

Although I padded all hard landing spots throughout the house, County suffered from very sore feet in her early years (right).

In her manic drive for threads as
nesting material, nothing escaped
County's searching eye (above).

Against sunlit blossoms, County's crest
feathers are raised in a joyful welcoming of spring, the season so traditionally associated with robins (left).

Towne's earnest, endearing charm
when she arrived—one week old
(left inset).

County's most peaceful baths
occurred when mischievous Towne
was indisposed with one of her
headaches (right).

Selecting materials for nest building (above left).

County chose a large, whitened cowskull with broad, solid horns (left) and packed the mud into the nest walls with her feet, her wings braced on the rim (above).

eyeing the last slice of toast, (one of her favourite foods) which the guest was still eating.

"Let her have a bit," I coaxed.

"She can have some when I'm finished," was the reply, followed immediately by crunching. County watched each bite with growing anxiety.

"Oh come, just give her a little piece."

"No, she can wait till I'm finished. Then she can have the last little bit."

But as the toast finally dimished to a small piece of crust, which was raised for the final bite, County could stand it no longer. Leaping onto the hand that dared to deny her, she snatched up the toast and swooped out of the room with it clutched triumphantly in her beak, verbal waves of indignation bubbling in her wake.

CHRISTMASTIME for County sparkled with new experiences—and opportunities for mischief. Oddly enough, the dramatic appearance of a spruce tree in the livingroom didn't intrigue her nearly as much as the melting snow that dripped steadily from it, spreading in tasty little wading pools underneath. The ornaments, too, she ignored, but she greatly enjoyed swooping the lighted candles on the branches—or perhaps it was my immediate consternation she enjoyed. Clementine oranges were a real treat, and pounding the sections into bitesize pieces that could be swallowed provided all the fun of a game for her. Fancy cookies and tarts left unguarded were discovered later dimpled with little excavations and surrounded by a sea of crumbs. Worm-like ribbons on presents under the tree were tugged loose, and anything wrapped in soft tissue paper just wasn't a secret any longer. Grapes in fruit-bowl arrangements were hammered into highly-unappetizing pulpy distortions, and decorative boughs and berries on windowsills scattered ruthlessly. Our house would *not* have been selected for the Christmas issue of a home decorating magazine.

County hadn't the extreme reserve around other people

during that first holiday season that developed over the following winter. A small gathering of friends found her mingling as easily as any other hostess, if perhaps more freely—joining a child on the floor in drawing pictures, tugging at chest hair in someone's open collar, helping herself to everyone's food. Knowing that I still have most of these people as friends is a standing tribute to their goodnature—to say nothing of their forbearance.

That same winter I had four very tame,lovable ducks outside. During one especially-severe cold spell, I brought them in each night, bedding them down cozily with hay inside the woodbox as I had done in previous years. In true duck fashion, they were always highly excited at these times, peering out in great glee, quacking incessantly and eager for the treats and hugs to come. During these visits it was one of their greatest delights to be sprayed with a plant mister, in compensation for the indoor dryness. They'd cluster around grabbing and gabbling enthusiastically at the spray as it beaded up on their heads and ran in rivulets down their throats, inside and out. County was highly intrigued, hopping along the edge of the woodbox, and my directing the odd quick jet at her as she bounced about caused considerable diversion and merriment for all. The ducks were puzzled by her boldness though, and eyed her doubtfully, not accustomed to being eye-to-eye with a fearless songbird wholly unintimidated by the close proximity of creatures several times larger than herself. Occasionally one would cautiously stretch his neck up behind County's back to poke hesitantly at her tail, which would startle her straight upwards, barking loudly, and startle all the ducks back down into the box in gabbling, trampling confusion. But eventually, following the lengthy games and salutations, she'd sit on the edge of the box preening while they preened too, or lay drowsily in the hay basking in warmth.

DURING that first winter, County gradually impressed upon me her need for earth indoors. When she arrived, I had a few potted plants on windowsills but, out of compassion, I gave nearly all of them away after County had repeatedly unearthed them. Finally, I began to consider that robins in the wild would swallow any earth clinging to bugs or worms they'd dig up, and that therefore earth is probably essential to their digestion, much as grit is to ducks and other birds who swallow much harder foods—teeth not being standard equipment. So as soon as the earth became visible in the spring, I dumped some into a large shallow box in the living room. County needed no invitation, and within seconds had sunk her toes with obvious enjoyment deep into the fresh damp dirt and was prodding eagerly for bugs. I then began to keep a dirt box always available for her, on a thick island of newspapers. County would drive her opened bill deep into the earth, repeatedly flicking aside mouthfuls in her digging frenzies, with the result that quite a huge radius of dirt was cast over the floor and then easily tracked everywhere.

Although this was just more mess to my eyes, it meant a larger area of dirt to County, and spending a lot of time in damp earth was also healthier for her feet. They simply were not designed for running or landing on dry hard surfaces, in particular, sharp right-angled edges, which are scarce in the wild.

Birds can become very lame if confined to hard, unnatural conditions, whether floors or perches. So all hard edges throughout the house wherever she might consider landing, had to be padded, adding a touch of mystique to the interior decor. As it was, County gradually developed very sore feet which were so painful that she'd sit on my shoulder with tiny sounds of pain whenever I shifted, since she couldn't grasp properly. During her worst periods, she spent each night on the side of my head as I lay in bed, perhaps also easing her discomfort with my warmth. She endured two or three weeks of this mysterious inflammation which I treated desperately with tetracycline, an antibiotic particularly helpful to birds. She then had two or three painfree months before being smitten again. The whole ordeal lasted at least two years, and although no vet could pinpoint the cause, I redoubled my efforts to soften hard surfaces everywhere in case they were the root of the problem. Her legs thickened over this period of time to twice the natural size, but a year after her last session of pain the entire encrustation on each leg came off in a single piece. Her legs resumed a normal appearance. Over the next two years they gradually thickened again, but apparently pain-lessly. The final cessation of foot problems coincided with the removal of lean ground meat from her diet and the substitution of live food instead. The whole situation remained riddled with mystery for me, and we were both very grateful when it was past.

DURING the migratory period of our first autumn together, I didn't notice any unusual excitement with County. The following spring, though, she became very high-strung and energized for at least a fortnight, and increasingly nervous around other humans—she'd even fly all night about the house whistling excitedly. It seemed as if she were unable to use up all her energy throughout the day during this metabolic upheaval and it just had to burst out during the night as well. Robins are usually day-time migrants; County however, was *always* active night and day during these seasons, napping only when necessary. As was I.

Anxious that she might hurt herself blundering about in the dark, I began leaving a light or two switched on all night downstairs, so she could fly in safety. However, this also enabled her to locate me easily, and she would frequently thump down on my head, with a surprising heaviness suggestive of a pair of ski boots, while I tried fruitlessly to sleep. With my bed being in a small loft over the high-ceilinged living room, I would hear her toenails tap-tap-tapping from the bottom of the stairs, up one step at a time to the top, followed by a pause; then a thump onto the bed-side table, a thump onto my head, then a series of hops down my side to my hip from which she'd launch herself (rather unflatter-ingly to me) out over the living room with shrill whistles and bizarre flying maneuvers—some absolutely vertical—only to be followed, over and over again, by tap-tap-tapping up the stairs. It was not a restful time of year, for *either* of us...

County's unusual migration whistles were intensely loud and extremely varied—reminiscent of a cockatiel—and she never used them in winter or summer. Neither have I heard them from wild robins, but perhaps they would only be needed during actual migratory flying—for encouragement and camaraderie, and maybe even guidance.

At the windows, with County, I'd constantly be watching for the arrival of exhausted migrants and worrying through the inevitable weather setbacks with an ever-increasing anxiety. The feeders were stocked year-round so there was always food waiting. Lying in bed and watching County's astonishing night flights under dusky conditions would set me musing about outside night migrants, like the tiny black and white warblers, who courageously fly through darkness against tremendous odds of survival, *for* survival, perhaps even passing overhead at that moment. Close companionship with one migrant can heighten one's concern for all of them; twice a year a large part of me has become deeply involved in the peril and drive of these awesome treks.

The persistence of our environmental decimation, as expressed in facts and figures, becomes even more embittering as one views it in terms of the increasing *unnecessary* hardships and perils for those innocent of causing them. I would have visions of our guardian spiritbirds spiraling onward through the threshold of brilliance, abandoning us to the retribution of our own darkness and ignorance.

CHAPTER THREE

COMPANIONSHIP

IN EARLY SUMMER OF THE YEAR that found County a year old, a second robin fledgling was brought to me whom I dubbed Towne, in a moment of inexcusable weakness, believing (once again) that she would be only a temporary inmate. However, Towne stayed and the name, embarrassingly, stuck. She arrived when she was seven or eight days old, exhausted and hungry, and after a good feeding nestled down on a towel in a small quiet box, turned her head back over her side like a little calf and slept soundly.

County, although interested, ignored Towne initially and contented herself with rummaging the container of worms I laboriously gathered early each morning. Not liking earthworms herself, contrary to popular belief about robins, she wickedly seized every opportunity to scatter Towne's worms everywhere. Nor would Towne eat earthworms after another week when given the choice, although she highly enjoyed tugging on worm-like fringes or fraying materials in play. Earthworms, it seemed, were for nestlings, and only if there was nothing else. In desperation that first winter, I had been feeding County raw lean ground beef with added vitamin drops and a dusting of brewers yeast—in addition to cheese, fresh fruit, tofu, currants, and my own food, which as luck would have it for her, is vegetarian. Towne quickly adapted to this diet, varied now by tantalizing contributions from a new mealworm culture I had just established. At this time too, County's sore feet began to heal, causing me to connect her problem with beef and its controversial contents. But County and Towne both refused any more beef after the arrival of the mealworms—wriggly protein was their uncompromising choice.

During the first few days that Towne was with us, I noticed a swelling towards the front of her left eye. As it reddened and seemed to be peaking, I lightly scratched it, thinking that perhaps some infected matter was being ejected. To my horror, inside was a wriggling larva of a parasitic fly which I promptly and gently removed with forceps. The wound healed almost immediately, but Towne's left eye quickly became blind and never grew to its full size.

For about the first week, Towne slept snugly at night on thick towels inside a draped box which had a lamp directed against the outside to warm the interior, the same arrangement I'd used with County. Then she began to roost in various places, one favourite spot being inside the cavity of a whitened cow pelvis hanging on the wall. Her tiny form nestled within that rigid bone softened the weathered austerity with a counterpoise of freshness and fragility—an embodiment of beginnings and endings.

As her confidence grew, Towne would try to join County and me in our various activities, flying inexpertly in our wakes, skidding along floors and off tables, and blundering into even the most unlikely objects with the unfailing accuracy of predestination. Her imperfect vision, in combination with her engaging adolescence and avid curiosity, called for nearly constant surveillance, mere foresight proving hopelessly inadequate. One day I really almost felt as though I had lifted the lid off the blender expressly for Towne to flop down instantly into a freshly-spun milkshake, only to get plucked out white, frothy, and totally upset. County tolerated Towne's enthusiastic comradeship, but rigidly enforced the dominance of the pecking order and the unseen boundaries of her own personal space—rules of behaviour which probably became particularly important when sharing the unchanging territory of a small house. If County sat on my head in the morning when I was still in bed, she would allow Towne to come no closer than my hip. But if Towne was the first to arrive, she'd be the one to pull my hair and eyelashes with unrelenting insistence. If I handed out food, or offered tidbits of my supper on the tip of my tongue, County insisted on being served first. She'd swoop at me if I offered first to Towne, driving Towne back to wait her 'proper' turn. When I'd sit in my armchair reading, with County on my shoulder, Towne would try repeatedly to sit on my unoccupied shoulder, only to be driven off each time by County. I would make no move whatever to resolve the dispute, having decided from the beginning to remain neutral when these situations arose. I knew that what Towne and County had to sort out was between robins and totally out of my range of understanding.

So they sorted it out. And I read.

Eventually, for reasons known only to them, Towne was occasionally permitted to sit on one shoulder while County sat on the other. But when she wasn't, I'd find myself rereading each line in meaningless repetition amid the squeals and barks and rushes of a battle royal. However, when the three of us *did* settle down in peaceful communion, it was such a warming experience that I'd set aside my reading as utterly peripheral.

Towne's life, in contrast to County's, seemed riddled with difficulties and perplexities, mostly owing to her impaired depth perception. She developed a chronically earnest and anxious expression, due to her perpetual clumsiness, which aroused immediate sympathy. Her frustration in trying to catch bugs released in the house was sorely aggravated by seeing County catch them with nimble dexterity instead. Towne would snap repeatedly at flies released in the window areas, catching perhaps one to County's six. Sometimes she would just sit by with a dejected air while County gobbled them up with ease and precision. Only then would I desert my neutral position and catch a few for her which she always accepted with resignation. But when she did catch something herself that was particularly succulent, like a slow-moving spider, she'd hold it tightly in her beak with little high whistles of excitement, setting it down and picking it up two or three times to savour the delight (while it wriggled helplessly and I looked elsewhere). But woe to her if County spotted this little ceremony. In a flash, she would swoop it up and zip off, to Towne's great dismay, while I conscientiously repressed my inclination to interfere. In her own brusque way, County was teaching Towne (albeit the hard way) to be immediate and efficient in disposing of meals. She was also indulging her own irrepressible devilishness.

But County's growing sympathy with her younger housemate shone out one day. I had gone for a walk in the woods for a couple of hours and when I returned, couldn't find Towne. A hurried search showed that she had somehow tumbled into a narrow space between a wall and a tall box and was unable to move. Heaven knows how long she'd been there. Sitting on the floor, I held her close for about an hour, trying to comfort her, for she was almost in shock. For a bird to be suddenly constricted and without free use of wings is a horrifying experience. Gradually she began to respond but chose to stay nestled in my hands, looking out with a subdued eye at County who periodically interrupted her usual activities to venture near, peering inquisitively at Towne. During one of these visits, she spotted a fair-sized spider on my shoe, pounced, incapacitated it expertly, and tossed it toward Towne. Towne stared at the spider, then at County, and back to the spider in disbelief. Then she edged down my lap towards it, stopping and looking at County again as though expecting her to snap it up. But County just watched without moving. Cautiously, Towne inched down to the floor and over to the spider, paused one last time to look enquiringly at County, and then carefully ate it. Afterwards the two of them flew off together. I sat perfectly still throughout this episode, utterly entranced.

Gradually Towne established herself in the household in a steady stream of charm and misadventure. She was overawed at first at the relative hugeness of Desmond and Molly, but eventually took to scooting daringly along their particular shelves, getting caught and shaken with distressing regularity while protesting shrilly. She never did develop County's cocky finesse in teasing them outright, and at times actually blundered right into them, paying dearly for her awkwardness. Perhaps, too, the pigeons' defensiveness was heightened by a year of County's teasing, which bore rather heavily on Towne in consequence.

During Towne's adolescence, I was still supplying a dirt box for County. But as County wouldn't let Towne investigate her box until it had been thoroughly picked over, *two* dirt boxes became necessary, stationed on opposite sides of the room. Even then, whenever I loaded them with fresh and wriggling earth, Towne would be so convinced that County was catching more than she, that she would repeatedly leave her own box to patter frantically across the floor to County's, only to be driven emphatically off. And—after giving her own box a preliminary rummaging, County would simply move in on Towne's, whose indignant objections she merely overruled. Even harder to witness was Towne's obvious delight in prodding her way through County's box when, since County was allowing her to do it, there would be very little left to find. Once again County, by way of her own insatiable appetite for bugs, was teaching Towne the necessity for quickness and efficiency whenever food was available—an essential lesson in the wild. The situation would be heightened to an insane pitch whenever I'd bring a jar of black ants (red ones were not accepted) into the house. I would shake some into County's box and she'd instantly pounce on them, pushing them among her feathers (which is part of the mysterious anting ritual followed by birds). Then she'd lie on them for short spells, with outspread wings and tailfeathers, thrusting yet more among her feathers before finally eating them all. While she was thus happily diverted, I would shake the rest of the ants into Towne's box and watch her eagerly pounce on them. But she'd be so convinced that County was getting more, and that she was somehow missing out again, that in spite of the squirming ants under her very toes, she'd tear off, after bolting down only a few, to keep watch over County's activities while ants swarmed up the sides of Towne's box, driving me to distraction. Not surprisingly, I eventually stopped bringing in ants. The wonder was that I was so naive as to have ever considered such a step in the first place.

By this time it had become evident that Towne's left eye would be a lifelong burden to her. She had painful headaches which were as obvious to discern as those of any human suffering the same malady. Even daylight would aggravate the pain at these times, and she'd roost in a dim, secluded spot until it eased. Although her spirits and appetite were always good, she also began to take strange seizures which I could only attribute to nerve damage from the larva. A sudden fright—like another human entering the house, the television being switched on (she never reconciled herself to that), or seeing a cat or hawk outside, would set her off, and she'd fly in a tight frenzied spin for several moments, her beak up like a pivot, then fall stunned to the floor. Sometimes I'd scoop her up to comfort her, but usually she would recover and fly off before I could reach her. Sometimes these seizures would happen at least once a day, sometimes weeks would pass without one. The problem called for a pre-planned lifestyle—visitors were covertly detoured to whatever part of the house Towne wasn't in at that moment to allow her to gradually become aware of their presence. Television viewings, fortunately rare anyway, were clandestinely indulged in behind closed doors. I even used caution changing my clothes, especially to any high-contrast colours or patterns, since even that had been known to set off a seizure. Towne (and the rest of us) seemed to oscillate between high-strung periods when any sudden change or move-ment had to be rigidly avoided, to periods of relative calm when activities could be more natural and relaxed. It was obvious that Towne could never return to the wild.

As SUMMER waned into autumn, both Towne and County moult-ed with Towne making the great change to adult female plumage, and both robins passed through highly-unflattering bristly stages, even becoming tailless for a time. They, as well as the pigeons (who seemed to moult with more dignity), spent the greater part of each day quietly engrossed in pulling out old feathers and tending the new, the falling feathers indoors echoing pleasantly the falling leaves outdoors, and tawny scatterings underfoot everywhere. It was a time of low-energy output, a lull before migration when batteries were recharged. They'd roost for hours out in the screened porch, preening, dozing and singing contentedly amid the mesmerising hum of late August crickets. But only County emerged with white wingbars.

They seemed to share a harmonious companionship, Towne accepting County's rank of seniority. Even when sitting at separate windows they would maintain a constant exchange of single high notes as they watched the outside world. They especially loved to do this at dusk as the light faded into darkening stillness under the trees with such a dignified decline that the switching on of an electric light came as an intrusion.

Hot sunny windowsills would coax them into wide-eyed, open-mouthed postures with feathers spread wide as they drank in the warmth and when they sang the 'cheerily-cheerily' robin song together, I realized yet again what a rare privilege it was to live with them. Interestingly enough, the close comradeship County and I had shared for a year was in no way diminished by the inclusion of Towne in the family circle—the aura simply widened to enclose all.

That summer was the first time that the screened porch also became a food trap. By leaving the light in it switched on all night and the doors open, great quantities of moths were attracted inside. Then, in the morning, I'd close those doors and open the door into the house where Towne and County would be impatiently pattering back and forth. The moment I'd open the door County would be through and snapping up moths in the porch, while star-crossed Towne as often as not would end up *behind* the opened door on the table by the window, unable to find her way out, and in anguish at seeing County getting moth after moth before her very eyes. Although I'd bundle her right out there, between her eyesight and her anxiety, she usually got the smaller share.

One day when Towne was in the livingroom, she spotted a moth fluttering around the legs of the wood stove. Instantly she scuttled over and caught it, but in juggling it around in her beak accidentally released it. It flitted silently past her blind eye and up to the window. Poor Towne searched all around the stove legs, but unable to find her moth, she turned away in resignation and suddenly spotted it at the window. Swooping up, she caught it and this time swallowed it. Then, perhaps heartened by her success, she returned to the stove area to hunt again for the 'other' one. Life was seldom easy for Towne.

As THE migratory season arrived, both robins gradually became high-strung and flighty, exchanging shrill whistles and barks and engaging in strange flying exploits at night. How awed I would be lying up in the loft in the middle of the night watching with wonder as two small friends repeatedly flew straight upwards in a perfect vertical, as though propelling themselves from a trampoline, then with a slight pause touch toes to the peak of the cathedral ceiling, before inverting, and flying straight downwards again. Sometimes they'd do it simultaneously; sometimes alternately in an intriguing ritual of mystery. The precision and speed accomplished under such subdued lighting week after week was amazing—especially with one of the participants handicapped with defective eyesight. Frequently, too, they'd swoop around the darkened loft at positively decapitating speeds for me (had I ever suddenly sat up), but with never a mishap. For a while, it almost seemed as though Towne flew better in the dark than in the light.

Autumn drew to a close, and I found myself faced with the difficulty not only of providing renewable dirt boxes throughout the winter months but also of coping with the endless messiness radiating from them. Out of this dilemma was born an indoor garden, about three feet by five, filled with damp earth and a selection of over-arching plants so dear to the hearts of secretive thrushes. Packaged potting soil was *not* used, and the edges of the boards were well padded to protect the birds' feet. Both robins were delighted with it, but County claimed it immediately as her own, which meant that Towne had to resort to sneaking in through the foliage at every opportunity and getting ignominiously booted out. It was all part of the fun, and they both enjoyed it tremendously, although an alarm call from an outside blue jay would instantly send them scurrying underneath the plants to hide, leaving an empty stage set with silence. With their woodland colouring amid the (almost) natural habitat they could both vanish completely and my utmost efforts could rarely detect them. But as the tension relaxed and the 'all clear' sounded outside, plants would suddenly 'blink' and two robins appear as if by magic.

As time went on, they began a curious rotating of the dominant role. For a number of weeks, County ruled as queen of the garden and house and Towne would decamp unquestioningly whenever County rushed at her. Then, for reasons I could never discover, there'd be a switch, and Towne would drive County off each time; County, to my unbounded astonishment, totally accepting the inferior position. Eventually, her period of dominance would come round again, only to give way again to Towne's.

To keep the garden interesting for them, I half-filled a few feed bags with earth and stored them in the porch, so that fresh dirt could be added to the garden every month throughout winter. Since it usually appeared as a large frozen lump that took a couple of days to thaw completely, the robins would have great fun helping it along by perching on the top and hammering at it like little woodpeckers. I added a lovely twist of driftwood as a lookoff (and a hide-under) and a large flat water-dish for bathing. I also tried the pleasing effect of a couple of squat candles at dusk among the foliage, but Towne showed such an otherwise laudable tenacity in grabbing persistently at the flames that I abandoned the idea. Often I would reflect that if it weren't for Towne and County and their need for earth, I might never have conceived of an indoor garden and the pleasure it gives. When snowstorms raged outside the windows overlooking the garden, and fluffed-up bluejays, sitting on the hanging vines of the Virginia creeper, stared in with fascination at 'summer,' I didn't wonder that gardenless people got 'cabin fever' in February. And when the newly-misted garden diffused the fragrance of a greenhouse through the living room, I was doubly grateful to the robins for enriching my life in yet another way.

FROM the beginning of Towne's mobility, County had made it clear that when she bathed, no other bird was to be near. This came as rather a surprise to me, since she'd never minded me. But Towne had to be driven nearly out of the room before County would turn her undivided attention to the bathing ritual. Naturally, having received this ultimatum, Towne resolved to provoke County every time she bathed, and County's most peaceful baths occurred when Towne was indisposed with one of her headaches. Sneaking back into the room and creeping through the garden shrubbery, Towne would inch as closely as the spying elders in biblical days while County, an irate Susanna, erupted out of the water and drove her off with outraged indignation. Again and again, Towne would devilishly stalk County in her bath regardless of being persistently routed, till finally a harassed County would seek what satisfaction she could in the briefest of watery flurries, retiring finally to preen somewhere in peace. It was useless for County to attempt retaliation, since Towne didn't mind in the least anyone being near when *she* bathed, but every once in a while County chased Towne, with seeming satisfaction, right out of her bath anyway.

WITH the passing of autumn came winter, heralded by the first firings of the wood stove—a major stumbling block for Towne, until she finally remembered, even at the peak of exciting activities, *not* to land on it. She came to avoid its presence altogether, and only rarely alternated with County in poising with spread feathers on the adjacent stack of firewood for a luxurious heat bath. But day by day, both robins would watch with crests raised in anticipation as I popped loose bark off each piece of firewood looking for tasty bark larvae underneath.

Although protected indoors from the fierce winter elements, all the birds still partook of the drama enacted on the other side of the windows, especially in the area of the feeding stations. Ruffed grouse and mourning doves would find Desmond and Molly particularly intriguing, and would perch on the nearest branches watching them with great attention. Sudden swooping attacks by sharp-shinned hawks glancing off the actual windows and scattering jays and juncos would send both robins and even at times the more imperturbable pigeons streaking out of the room in a panicky blur. Everyone would freeze at blue jay alarm calls, which were to be instantly heeded and never questioned. Whenever a hawk made a kill in front of the windows, the pigeons would crouch motionlessly and growl, staring with enormously-rounded eyes, while County would vanish to the upstairs closet for an indefinite period, and poor Towne, more likely than not would have a seizure followed by seclusion in the darkest spot she could find. I, meanwhile, would feel as if I had absorbed *all* their reactions combined. Even a placid barred owl, landing on a branch ten feet from the window, had everyone quite literally in a flutter, indoors and out, and cats always brought out growls in the pigeons and County's low cluck of alarm. Many times she has flown into a room where I was working, with that same low clucking and eyes earnest and anxious till I would go to the windows, spot the cat, run outside and chase it away. Then, contented again, she would return to whatever she was doing when she caught sight of the unwelcome intruder. Rabbits, squirrels, chipmunks and groundhogs caused very little concern when they appeared, but skunks, raccoons, porcupines, dogs and deer provoked considerable upheaval in the household. Cats, hawks, crows, ravens, and humans, however, led the field for distrust and disturbance, and sometimes I felt County could spot any one of them in pitch-darkness. If she was crouched utterly motionless in the garden sounding a tiny, high alarm note at intervals and I put my face down beside her, and peered up through the plants, through a corner of the mullioned window, through the clustering vines and arching tree branches outside, sure enough, I would see a tiny silhouette of a hawk circling slowly, at least half a mile or more away, within what appeared to be a square inch of sky.

CHAPTER FOUR
UPHEAVAL

THE SUMMER TOWNE TURNED ONE YEAR OLD and County two found yet another orphan in the family—a two-day-old duckling with a passion for nibbling on shoelaces. I christened him Busybill. The previous summer I had lost my other duck friends to wild predators (not for the first time) and had sworn that it wouldn't happen again. So Busybill lived indoors with the rest of us. He had a little pen bedded with wood shavings and containing a sink for bathing, and although he was a little messier, his needs and ours could be accommodated with a little foresight, drawing heavily on years of experience with outside ducks. He loved going for walks and truck rides, stopping at creeks and lakes for a swim. He vied with the robins for treats in the kitchen, and would respond with thudding webs and eager quacks to the opening of the fridge door even from the other end of the house. Anything edible that fell on the floor disappeared instantly down Busy's throat, and beetles that failed to interest the robins were his. Like any duck, he loved water in all forms, whether from a defrosting fridge, a thawing Christmas tree, or snowcovered boots; he positively insisted on sharing the shower. He learned that the robins' garden was off-limits, at least whenever anyone was looking, but he also developed a contradictory taste for the supplies of cheese and currants he *found* in their garden.

Towne and County tolerated the ever-bustling Busybill with remarkable calm—and perhaps even a hint of contempt. He, too, heeded the alarm calls issued regularly by the jays outside and of even greater note, reacted with considerable fear and trepidation, when he was only about three weeks old, to hearing muffled shots from duck hunters at the lake nearly a mile away.

As moulting time came round again with all five changing their plumage, the floors would be intricately patterned with feathers, white and iridescent brown from the pidgies, white, gray, russet and black from the robins, and greenish-black, white and gold from Busybill.

THAT Christmas Eve I was unexpectedly hospitalized, with surgery recommended within a few days. Friends rallied round, taking care of the birds until I was released from the hospital nearly two weeks later. Each day until the surgery when I'd phone home, County and Towne would gather near the phone, watching my friend speaking to me, only to fly off as soon as he hung up. He was unable to coax them to take food from him, although they would eat what he'd leave out for them. Busybill, bereft of his usual amount of attention, would enthusiastically drag at the visitor's shoelaces while following him around the house as he tended birds, watered plants, loaded the wood stove, and dealt with numerous other tasks. On the morning of the operation, an ordeal I'd never faced before, my friend tried to gather all the birds around him to help in transmitting an aura of reassurance to me. But no one would cooperate and he finally gave up and sat down in my usual armchair. Then shortly after ten o'clock, Molly flew up over his head, settled herself on a shelf, and began a long calling-coo, over and over. Gradually all the birds gathered around on their favourite roosts, and Busy coaxed till he was lifted up into my friend's lap.

Meanwhile, at ten-fifteen, as the anesthetic was flowing into my arm and the anesthetist was kindly suggesting that I turn my fast-numbing thoughts towards whatever would make me feel happiest, I thought instantly of the birds—if indeed I had ever stopped thinking of them. My fear vanished, and I felt as if I were buoyed up on a cloud.

At that same moment, all the birds became perfectly still and remained so for the next twenty-five minutes—the actual length of the operation—before bestirring themselves again.

Comparing notes later with my friend allowed us to discover this miraculous connection, this invisible bond of support.

It was wonderful to have had such support—and even more wonderful returning home again to them for healing.

THE following spring saw a gradual increase of tension in our household. Towne was enduring more and more seizures and headaches, which kept her unusually high-strung (which in itself may have rendered her susceptible to more). Almost anything would set off a seizure: toast popping up from a toaster, the sudden ring of the telephone, the schoolbus passing the windows, the sight of a laundry basket in my arms. She and County were quite high-strung at this time anyway and on the go day and night with erratic migratory flights and whistles. Meanwhile, Busybill was maturing into a very determined drake with decidedly aggressive tendencies, and would rush menacingly with lowered outstretched neck at any bird upon 'his' floors. He also actively resented my showing affection towards the other birds, and County in particular. This became so worrisome that I was driven finally to introduce him into a flock of neighbouring pond ducks which, thankfully, he eventually enjoyed. The possibility of his unrestrainable aggression being directed at Towne when she was helplessly recovering from a seizure on the floor was too appalling to be chanced. Injections to balance his belligerent hormonal upheavals had failed to soothe him, and Towne certainly couldn't be released. Poor Busybill's hormones were just incompatible with the rest of the household, and his departure left mingled emotions of regret and relief.

A few weeks later, when I had been out for an afternoon, I returned home to find Towne dead on the floor, in all probability the result of a final seizure. Sadly holding her in my hands while County sat quietly on my shoulder, I gently stroked her and laid my face against her soft plumage, noticing the beauty and perfection of each feather. I pitied her for the suffering she'd had to endure throughout the two years of her short life, and I was humbled by her admirable spirit, which had enabled her to extract so much enjoyment out of each day in spite of continual setbacks. I buried her just ouside the window beneath a white birch tree, the tree by which, traditionally, the ancient shamans, those visionary healers, ascended to the Light to intercede on behalf of the earthbound. County, bereft, slept for several nights nestled on the side of my head as she had been wont to do during her own times of pain.

CHAPTER FIVE

SPRING SONG

ABOUT A MONTH AFTER TOWNE'S PASSING, County, in addition to her usual high spring energies began to express very strong nesting urges. Each day she frantically gathered beakloads of hair and strips of paper from all over the house and flew constantly to the windows with them, eyeing the outside robins with totally new regard and calling to them continually. She even managed one day to bloody her feet, whether in desperately shredding the paper towels in the holder or in scratching at the windows, I was unable to determine. But I saw with dismay that I would have to offer her the wild heritage that hadn't been hers for the past three years. The loss of such a marvellous companion as County would be an ordeal but there was no choice. Her happiness and welfare were my trust. So one morning in May, when she was out in the screened porch, I quelled my personal resistance, opened the door, stood aside, and with voice and gesture offered her the world of the wilderness. At first she was startled and drew back. But after a few moments she hopped along the table right up to the open doorway and stood looking out. It was a beautiful sunny morning, and a handsome male robin was foraging in the grass. A small breeze stirred, and the sunlight twinkled tantalizingly through the young leaves of the trees. County paused, scratched her head, looked out again, looked at me, and then flew—back into the house. I could hardly believe my eyes. Directly after that momentous decision, County shared the full robin courtship rituals with me, as with a chosen robin spouse, and settled down in earnest to build her first nest. I settled down in earnest to fulfill the role of a male robin spouse, a formidable challenge in itself.

With a real genius for adapting the unusual to the suitable in her selection of nesting material, she rummaged the entire house, pounding her findings into malleable limpness and mingling them with damp earth from the garden. To make clear to me the need for stickier mud, she carried beakloads of dirt over to the kitchen sink area and soaked them in any available water lying around till the whole counter was crisscrossed into a maze of muddy tracks and bits of soggy paper. Even yet, I can open my recipe book to a double spread of indelible robin footprints. I took the hint and wetted some of the garden earth to the desired consistency.

Her energy was boundless, and *nothing* escaped her searching eye. An unguarded tag and string dangling from an immersed tea bag was instantly seized and tugged, with imminent peril of scalding. A neat little pile of receipts not yet entered into the tax ledger was raided, and pounded out of all useful recognition into muddy pliability. I can only hope for leniency if I'm ever audited.

Shopping lists magnetized to the fridge went the way of the receipts, and I found myself blocking aisles while hopelessly scrutinizing muddy scrawls in the midst of bustling grocery stores. Couch cushions were harassed mercilessly into releasing their fringes, and paper towels and toilet rolls were shredded so consistently that I finally bolted them into the cupboards. Even the paper in a Japanese sliding screen door was recognized for its nest-building possibilities and torn out ruthlessly in strips. Any fabric that showed the least inclination to fray, including whatever I chanced to be wearing, was badgered ceaselessly into yielding its particular contribution. As soon as I stepped out of my clothes to shower, County stepped into them, tugging frenziedly on any trailing threads or loose elastic. Even the towel I groped for afterward had her worrying the frayed edge at the other end. One result of being taught to see my surroundings for their nest-building potential was that I quickly came to realize how shabby everything had been getting—to say nothing of the shabbiness to which we were rapidly tending. At that point, I began to do what a male robin would have done long ago, and brought her quantities of damp dead grass, twigs, and trailing lichens from the spruce trees, which County welcomed enthusiastically. Only then did the nest really begin to take shape.

The site she selected for her architectural pursuits might seem bizarre from a human's viewpoint, but from that of an indoor robin to whom trees were not available, it was unquestionably sound. She chose a large whitened cowskull with broad solid horns. The skull hung on the wall close to a raftered ceiling, which gave a sense of inaccessibility and privacy, important considerations. At the top, behind the horns, was a level spot just nest-sized. From it she could command a wide view of her domain and even out beyond the windows, none of which were uncomfortably close, while the horns provided excellent landing bars not only for her, but for the babes to come; all in all, a very secure pivot for those vulnerable nesting activities soon to unfold.

When the initial accumulations of muddy twigs, paper, threads, and grasses refused to stick as a unit but persisted in crumbling away at the edges, I stuck some stiff, dense spruce branches, devoid of hazardous needles, into the skull cavities surrounding the nest and bound them there tightly with twine. That helped immensely, and the nest grew quickly. The branches gave a more natural feel, too, and even more privacy when brooding time came.

How did County know the procedure for building a nest? How did she know which materials would be suitable, especially when some were extracted from a human environment, and yet served just as well? How did she know which of the materials I offered her to refuse? How did she know the proper consistency of the mud? She had never seen a nest built, and neither had I. I had the 'advantage' in that I had at least read about it—and yet it was she who knew how to do it precisely. 'Instinct' is such an easy answer for us, and like other easy answers, explains little.

As the nest grew, I tried to fulfill my role in bringing County beakful quantities of grasses and small amounts of mud while she shaped and reshaped the cavity to her satisfaction. Poring through bird books, and gathering particular lichens and other mosses cited as favoured by robins in nest-building, I would proudly hold up my selections to her, only to see her glare at them balefully, seize and fly off with them, and drop them in another room before returning to her work. Her refusals were as emphatic as her acceptances were gentle. Another of my ploys met with greater success—I gave her an old nest I'd treasured for years, which she demolished and happily incorporated.

I'd often wondered how birds rounded the inside walls of their nests with such perfection using only their mouths and feet, and County gave me the answer. She'd lie down in her nest with her wings spread a little forward so that her breast was against the wall and each wing was braced at the 'wrist' on the top rim of the nest. Then she'd paddle her feet very rapidly against the wall directly behind her, packing the mud and grasses tightly together. A pause, and she'd stand up, turn slightly sunwise and look at me speakingly. I would immediately respond by dropping a little mud under her tail. Then she'd lie down in her former posture, drumming the new mud into the wall behind her in the area adjacent to the former. With repeated additions of mud, and her gradually revolving body harmonizing with the flow of the macrocosmos, the nest, a microcosmos, grew higher, stronger and beautifully circular. I always knew whenever I missed the signal for grass instead of mud, because she would seize the unwanted lump, fly off and drop it in another room. Then she'd return with a mouthful of individually-selected grasses, all lying crosswise in her beak, shake them out right and left in the nest, hop in, and resume her paddling movements. Of course I would immediately replace my mud contributions with grass instead, four or five aligned blades at a time like a robin would carry, until we made the switch back to mud, another signal I usually missed. All this involved hours of constant application for County (and me). She rarely snatched a moment to eat unless I offered her something, which she only occasionally took time to accept. Once, at least, she indulged in a quick bath to dislodge the ever-accumulating mud encrusting her feet and breast. It was with a feeling of embarrassment that I decided I simply had to have a sustaining cup of tea and some food—which I bolted down defensively.

One strenuous day of ecstatic unflagging labour after the definitive building process had begun found a virtually completed nest with only the lining lacking. Day's end found an exhausted robin with just enough energy left to clean herself and retire to her inconvenient roost on the shower rod, and an equally exhausted (though with less reason) human in equally-muddy attire but with no hope of a shower till the morning, and a living room comprehensively spattered and bedraggled with clods of mud, bits of twigs, sodden paper, lichen, brown puddles, muddy tangles of dead grass, smeary footprints in all directions (both human and avian), and a large flat dish of brown water from County's final bath. An hour and a half of concentrated cleaning and then I, too, was ready, thankfully, to roost.

COURTSHIP with County began a week before I opened the door to her, and about ten days before building the nest. She'd greet me with a little special pacing to and fro, tiny warbles spilling out from her open poised beak. But the full ritual wasn't expressed until she finally chose to stay with me. Early each morning, as soon as it was light enough for her to find me, she'd fly to my pillow awakening me with the special notes and actions of a female robin spouse, to which I tried to respond appropriately. She would pace in a carefully-measured tread back and forth before my face eyeing me with rounded eyes, her beak and tail up at about forty-five degree angles, her mouth fixed open with tongue standing up, and muted high-pitched warbles trilling forth with delightful variety. She would also do some bowing right and left, and circling, while still singing and pacing evenly. I found in responding to her entrancing overtures that she liked to be stroked very gently—a gesture she'd ordinarily decline—and usually when I did so, she'd stop and crouch slightly, encouraging pressure slowly down her back before she resumed pacing. When she'd crouch with tiny, high short notes, shiver her wings a little and raise her tail, I'd press firmly down along her back with my hand and then gently pull along the length of her tail with my thumb on top and fingers below. Often I would lay my cheek against her back, whispering softly to her as she sang. After several minutes of courting, County would carry on with the day's activities interrupting them occasionally for more courting when she felt the need. If I had to leave the house for several hours, I was met on my return with courtship overtures heavily imbued with anxiety—as would be natural between two mated robins, so long a separation being considerable cause for alarm. So I tried to avoid distressing her with prolonged absences.

The day following the building of the nest, County continually examined every square inch of floor and carpet, collecting fine hair and lint suitable for lining the nest. Throughout the day she carefully moulded them into a soft woven cup with her feet. Pulling hairs gently out of my head, I would align them and offer them to her as she busied herself at the nest, taking pleasure in her solemn acceptance as she reached out to grasp them and tuck them beneath, paddling them back with her feet. By the end of the day the nest was completely finished, and the new lining now awaited the eggs. That night, happily absorbed in her maternal anticipations, County abandoned the shower rod roost and slept for the first time in a nest of her own making.

Most of the following morning she spent in the nest with laboured breathing. I missed the actual laying of her first egg, which must have taken place in the adjoining room since later I found a broken soft-shelled egg there beneath a window perch. By late afternoon County's subdued spirits had arisen again and her discomfort must have lessened, allowing her natural liveliness to return. By the following mid-morning, her breathing was slow and laboured again with a small grunt between each breath. At noon she stood on the edge of the nest with her tail over the cup, and with long breathed-out efforts slowly pushed her egg out into the nest. But again, it was extremely thin-shelled and broke when it fell. I removed it immediately, and she lay down in the nest for a long quiet rest. By late afternoon, her spirits and liveliness had again returned and she began to indulge an unheard-of craving for bananas—even hammering holes in unpeeled ones when the minced offerings I set out for her were eaten. The third egg (which came the third day) seemed to give her the most pain of all, her panting and grunting being easily heard twenty feet away. I was terribly worried that the egg would break inside her and indeed this was the case. When I found it a day or two later it was a tightly compressed 'dropping' of crushed blue. Her appetite that day was ferocious, and by nightfall, she again became livelier. I began to wonder if the supply of bananas was going to hold out. The fourth egg arrived the following afternoon with much less discomfort and, thankfully, this one was sound. I felt as though I, too, could finally breathe easier now. Oddly enough, she never cared for bananas again.

Day after day County cared for her surviving egg, warming it, turning it, moistening it as necessary with bath-dampened feathers and when her mothering hopes got ahead of her, even carrying food up to it and clucking hopefully. The outside birds, too, were busy with nesting activities and territorial disagreements and whenever one would land near the windows, especially a jay, County would zoom off her nest and bounce down at the window in a belligerent explosion of bristling feathers and staccato beak-snapping. She made it perfectly clear that I, too, was to defend the nest, so I would instantly join her, shouting at the 'intruder,' tapping on the window and snapping my teeth in lieu of a beak, (causing considerable astonishment outdoors since after years of my stocking the feeders, the jays in particular had acquired a much milder impression of me). Even Desmond and Molly, flying blissfully past the camouflaged nest on their way to the upstairs loft, were attacked in mid-flight by an outraged County who swooped and kicked at them unremittingly, to their utter bewilderment. To keep the peace I had to restrict their activities to the other end of the house with an improvised barrier which, fortunately, they accepted graciously. Otherwise, my daily labours centred upon conscience-riddled hunts for a wild robin's nest from which I hoped to clandestinely extract one egg—after all, my responsibilities as a father robin included the understanding that I could fertilize eggs.

ROBIN nests, beautifully camouflaged within dense spruce foliage are, not surprisingly, difficult to detect, in spite of the alarmed barks of the parents betraying the proximity of a nest. Days of chilly, concentrated searching during the most drizzly of spring weather revealed only two nests, within acres of wild woodland heavily populated with robins. One was very difficult to reach and had babies nearly fledged. The other, though, was only fifty feet from the house, six feet above the ground, and had young-sters naked and still blind. As quickly and unobtrusively as possi-ble, one was gently removed. Within moments the female had fluttered back down over her remaining chicks while I sped back to the house, a tiny life so vital to County's happiness held warm-ly next to my skin, and a load of unavoidable guilt on my heart. As soon as I entered the livingroom, I scattered some mealworms on the floor. When County swooped down to them hungrily, I immediately replaced her egg with the baby. Then I called excit-edly to her to come back up to the nest. Alighting on the rim, she stared in awe at the little wriggling creature struggling to lift its head, while I prattled on as enthusiastically as any other new father. Eyeing the baby and me in turn for several long moments, she gradually began to lower her brooding feathers, paused, and finally stepped into the nest, snuggling down protectively over him. An expression which I had never seen before filled her eyes. County was a mother at last, and parenthood had begun—for both of us.

LATER that evening, as I watched them learning about each other in a nest woven into a skull, I marvelled at the richness resonating before me: the skull, whitened into an unearthly beauty through the intervention of death—a life taken without leave, the centre desecrated by a bullet hole—with its impotent horns of defense gently cradling a new beginning of unfolding innocence; the minglings of the terrestrial and the celestial, the interweaving of Life and Death.

CHAPTER SIX

PARENTING

My FIRST CONCERN WAS HOW WE'D EVER GET THE BABE to gape since he was unable yet to see food coming, but County had that problem well in hand. With a mealworm in her beak, she uttered a low cluck from deep within her throat, and instantly, the nestling's neck shot straight up and his mouth opened wide. But because he was a single chick in the relative roominess of the nest and without support from siblings, he wobbled about erratically, gaping hungrily, while County tried repeatedly to position her beakful of food over his weaving mouth. Finally, I held him still with my fingers gently encircling his head, and County thrust the mealworm deep into his throat.

From that moment, an intense preoccupation with the habits of insects pervaded my summer days—and even invaded my dreams at night where I would clutch wildly at diaphanous worms. Feedings were necessary every fifteen to twenty minutes for the nestling from 5:30 a.m. till about 9:30 p.m., and County herself wanted live food all day, in addition to fruit and cheese. So daily I donned rubber boots, mitts, raincoat, and insect net to plunge reluctantly into shrill clouds of voracious mosquitos that sought (and found) gaps in my armour as I crouched by the hour, turning over logs, old boards, and rocks, and sorted with gritted teeth through decomposing compost looking for insects to fill my bucket. My daily aim was to keep a large pan of insects readily available for County to hunt through for the baby as well as for herself. She would do the feedings and I would provide the food. Mostly I returned with flat brown centipedes, sowbugs, bark larvae, spiders, caterpillars, earthworms and those which defied categorization and which I tried to grab without giving myself time to shudder. If I didn't know what they were, let alone if they were edible, I could always trust County's judgment. A wriggling pink-and-yellow something, studded with clumps of black bristles was not my idea of food. Perhaps it was just a cultural difference.

Bugs collected during a two or three hours search in the morning, combined with moths trapped overnight in the screened porch, and the ebb and flow of the mealworm culture, would get us through each day—and amply reinforce my vegetarian commitment. Of course, escapees throughout the house were inevitable, and necessitated a careful step, but I soon became accustomed to shaking out my shoes before putting them on and checking through the blankets before climbing into bed. The continual procession of multi-legged creatures lured into the house each day bore a disturbing resemblance to those I used to ignominiously eject. Fatherhood had enhanced them considerably in my eyes.

Just as she had known exactly how to build a nest, County knew exactly how to care for her young. Later experience helped me to ascertain that her first nestling must have been about three days old when he arrived, eyes still unopened and his pink skin showing dark patches where the first feathers were ready to emerge. County not only warmed him, but daily pierced the bottom of the nest in several places with her beak and vibrated it vigorously—perhaps lessening the immediate density, so that the warmth radiating from her brooding patch, a featherless 'heating pad' on her belly where the feathers parted, could circulate around the baby into the holes below rather than just heating him on top. She would also stand back and touch him two or three times with the tip of her sensitive beak, pausing thoughtfully after each touch as though considering his body temperature; perhaps, too, his rhythms or reflexes. They were gestures of seeming importance in regulating his care, and were repeated daily until he was feathered. If he was in an unsuitable position to be brooded, perhaps with his neck twisted back, she would poke him sharply until he squirmed around. If the new position was satisfactory, she would step in with lowered feathers and wriggle herself down over him contentedly. Again, that indescribable expression would fill her eyes.

THE DROPPINGS of young robins are very tidy in the beginning. At nearly every feeding, as soon as the food is swallowed, the youngster lowers his head and pushes up his rump to eject a dropping of loose consistency encased in a transparent casing. This sac allows the parent to seize the dropping without it dripping, and to carry it away before discarding it, thus preventing telltale fecal buildup near the nest. There is no odour either, unless the sac is broken open, and perhaps no taste, since I noticed that County often just swallowed them hastily when her duties were rushed. Perhaps, if there is a taste, this gave her another way of monitoring his progress. Initially too, the vent (or anus) is on top of the rump, just back of a tiny stub which later becomes a tail. With three or four babies crowding a nest, these upward-facing vents are an obvious convenience for everyone, but as the nestling grows larger and longer and the tail begins to protrude, the vent is gradually repositioned underneath, as in the adult. By about ten days of age, when the fledgling is out of the nest, his vent is below, and his now-sacless droppings are entirely his own concern.

In an amazingly short time, the little one's feathers began to emerge like tiny spikes, the outer casing of which crumbled away with preening, allowing the feathers inside to open. It seemed as though they grew a quarter-inch each day. Simultaneously (time being of the essence in the wild), the slits in the bulbous closed eyes quickly gained definition. Two days after he had arrived, County's babe opened his eyes and actually began to preen his tiny, tufted feather spikes. It is unlikely that his heritage had prepared him for the sight of such an unusual set of parents, but he must have taken it well in his stride, since he continued to grow at a pace which passed belief. Not only was he the sole recipient of food in the nest, he was the willing subject of County's unrestrained delight in feeding babies. Over the next few days, he grew like an inflating balloon, and his feathers seemed to visibly lengthen with each feeding. He preened them frequently, and began to beat his wings enthusiastically when being fed—a delightful gesture County herself often performed just briefly whenever she took tidbits from me, especially during nesting seasons. He also practiced standing (shakily) and wing-stretching (constantly), even getting his leg over his wing to scratch his head when he was a week old. Due to the ever-increasing demand for bugs in the family, and to my ever-increasing absorption in their supply, when turning over possible names for the baby my harassed thoughts could settle on nothing but bugs—so Bugs he was called. It was with mingled pride and amusement that I would inform select friends that although Bugs undoubtedly resembled his mother, he unquestionably got his size from me. With fitting repartée, I was sent a Father's Day card.

Of course, like any proud father, I had to have frequent recourse to photographs to prove just how unbiased and justified was my pride, but until he grew accustomed to it Bugs, standing and gazing innocently out of the nest, would instantly drop flat at the loud click of the camera. Perhaps it was too similar to the alarming outbursts of beak-snapping in which County conveyed territorial violations to the outside jays. A mother goat loosing a sudden loud snort of alarm will cause her young kid to instantly flatten himself down in the grass to hide; for me, the sudden click of supposedly solid lake ice under my feet will cause my own legs to immediately wobble. Fortunately, the clicking of the camera became too common to be noticed (and too exhausting to acknowledge each time), and since County never reinforced his alarms, the photos rapidly accumulated.

From the first, County had absolute trust in me handling her babe. I fed him occasionally too, and removed the fecal sac if she wasn't near, though if she saw me take it, she would in turn take it from me and dispose of it. Each day I lifted him gently out of the nest to photograph his progress, and not once did she ever indicate any distress at my actions. I reciprocated by not prolonging the outing. Nor did the camera in my hand alarm her. Once when I was trying unsuccessfully to coax Bugs into gaping for the food I was holding, County, standing by as I chirped futilely, clucked the single special note that opened his mouth each time and watched as I happily fed him. Her trust in me was as complete as though I were, indeed, another robin—to me, a most touching honour.

A WEEK to the day that his eyes opened Bugs flew for the first time. In his first effort, he hopped onto my head as I stood by the nest, but he slid about precariously, so I carefully replaced him. His eager curiosity was far from satiated, though, and next he flew daringly across the living room, crash-landing abruptly at the windows. Tail feathers are the last to lengthen, there being no room for them in the nest, and no need for them either, so as a result, Bugs had very little braking control, and nearly all his landings were dramatic. But his obvious delight in mobility was wonderful to watch as he skidded in excited bursts along the widowsills, blundered unfailingly into plants, and then careened awkwardly towards County who was nearby, avidly eating chokecherry blossoms. He tired quickly though, his legs being unused to supporting him constantly as yet, and he would often sit down rather suddenly and fall abruptly into a doze.

County now fed Bugs less frequently, taking food to wherever he happened to be, but as the time between feedings lengthened, our parenting duties changed. She had been indulging sporadically in the 'gathering' phase that precedes nest building, and two days after Bugs left the nest, she was frenziedly rebuilding on top of it in preparation for a second brood—to my considerable astonishment. I, on the other hand, was expected to assume more immediate reponsibility for Bugs' welfare, doing most of the feedings, teaching him to find and recognize natural food and to eat it himself—acting as a wild robin father would do at this point. The role of the father was made clear to me by County relinquishing a good deal of the role of the mother. Most of Bugs' hunger calls she ignored, leaving them to me, and I gamely hovered over him, dangling an inviting worm and chirping until my lips were rigid trying to coax him to gape. But Bugs, in great puzzlement, would watch the worm with less and less interest, and then, looking past me, would hop off to explore whatever caught his eye. In despair I would wave it about, swoop it towards him like County alighting on the nest with one, dip it in water letting a worm flavoured drop trickle in the side of his beak, and even tap him on the head with it as I'd seen County do once, before finally releasing the creature out of compassion. Very rarely could I coax open Bugs' mouth, and I knew that forcing it open wouldn't teach him how to take hold of food. By chance, I hit upon another method that promised well. Once, when Bugs was watching County taking pieces of grape off my tongue, I spontaneously offered grape to him the same way—and he took it. True, he stood a moment, surprised and undecided, with it tightly in his grip (and my excited imagination pushing it eagerly down his throat), but when I elevated his beak with the tip of my finger, he swallowed the grape. My jubilance knew no bounds. And although he didn't always cooperate, it was a beginning. But whenever I became absolutely frustrated by what during those times I termed his obstinance (in my calmer moments, his innocence), I would carry both him and the food over to County who was usually energetically gathering mud, and plead for her assistance. If she were so disposed, she'd drop a cluck in passing, and one puzzled crop would finally be filled.

Ours was a busy family. Mud in the garden had to be kept at the proper consistency, and fresh grass kept available as the new nest grew. I chose fresh rather than dead grass this time; dead grass had been predominant a few weeks earlier, so it had seemed a natural choice, but fresh grass was now abundant, so I argued that other robins would be using it as well. I certainly had no time to take a stroll to see if I was right in my surmise. In any case, County approved, and soon she was methodically inspecting the floors and carpets for lining material. At this point, I deliberately refrained from cleaning them for a couple of days, so that she could find enough strands of hair and other fine leavings (which were sprinkled liberally all over the house) for nest building. (I hoped, too, that under these deplorable housekeeping circumstances, no one except hardened friends would drop in unexpectedly for a visit.) County and I were also sharing our special courtship exchanges again in anticipation of another setting of eggs, and noisily defending our territory against other birds who ventured too near. Each night before retiring, I set the 'porch trap' for collecting moths, and about six o'clock every morning, while County was catching them for herself and Bugs, I'd set out, clad rather suffocatingly in the June warmth against mosquitos, to gather enough bugs for the day's feedings. Often I'd have to go out again in late afternoon if the morning's catch was insufficient. Otherwise, I was constantly occupied in teaching Bugs to catch his own food—with fluctuating results. One of my ploys (which was more successful than gyrating worms inscrutably before his eyes) was to lift him up, perched on my finger, to the moths fluttering against the screens inside the porch. Their quick movements did more than any of my previous efforts to stimulate him to seize his mealtime prey, but his progress was still slow—due unquestionably to my inadequate methods of instruction. At least now he greeted me with enthusiasm whenever I came in with a fresh load of his namesakes, and would sit on the rim of the bug box watching the wriggly inhabitants with considerable interest. At this point, with her nest ready and waiting for eggs, County, to my immeasurable relief, spent a single afternoon teaching Bugs herself. By evening he was picking up worms on his own. I sat humbly by, watching and marvelling—and, hopefully, learning as well.

CHAPTER SEVEN

FUN AND FOSTERING

EXACTLY A WEEK AFTER BUGS FLEW FOR THE FIRST TIME, County laid the first egg of the second clutch with another session of laboured breathing. The egg was sound. Within the next two days, County was happily brooding a clutch of three. Perhaps her previous difficulties were related to her first laying experience and were now behind her. Bugs frequently joined her at the nest, even brooding the eggs himself with tiny clucks as he settled down over them, but more often he just sat on the edge of the nest while County brooded. Once I photographed him bringing her food, which she accepted graciously; another time he plucked up the bottom of the nest for aeration and engaged in some of the footwork County used in forming the walls, and on another eye-opening occasion executed a little of County's courting move-ments on one of the horns while watching her on the floor below. It might have been supposed from some of these actions that Bugs was a female, but he didn't leave us until he was three and a half months of age — by that time he was already acquiring some of his brick red adult plumage which was unquestionably male. I had suspected that he was male when his nestling feathers came in; his head was very much darker, almost black really, as com-pared with Towne or County at that stage. Indeed, this proved to be a consistent indication of gender in young robins.

Days of intense brooding for a bird of County's natural liveli-ness seemed to necessitate a steady rotation of equally intense recreation. When break time came, she'd zoom off the nest with a loud "ka-ka-ka-ka-ka" which was earsplitting at close range. If I had seen this behaviour in the wild, I'd have assumed that it was intended to draw the attention of possible observers away from the nest. But I have never seen it. Perhaps for County it actually was just a vehement explosion of relief and high spirits, since it was invariably followed by the wildest games of her own invent-ing (which I've also yet to see in the wild).

She'd swoop me several times with exuberant shrieking just to get me motivated, in rather the same way as she used to stir up the pigeons. Once she had me feinting wild grabs at her, she'd ensconce herself under the huge piece of driftwood in the garden, or under a low table, with 'all her beaks' covering every exposure and the game would begin in earnest. I'd make repeated snatches at her tail with both hands from as many angles as possible and as fast as I could, while she simultaneously grabbed at my fingers, volleys of loud beak-snaps registering near-hits as well as cocky ultimatums. A score for me was when I actually grabbed her tail, dragged her out triumphantly and released her, after which she'd immediately scuttle back under the root. A score for her was when she grabbed a finger and was jerked out suddenly, attached like a lobster, only to let go and swoop off shrieking in great glee. Sometimes I started the game by creeping up on her with nefarious deliberation and trying to grab her tail while she was looking out the window. Then she'd leap up with a melodramatic shriek, swoosh down under the driftwood and the game was on. It was one of her favourite diversions during brooding times and it often left me on the floor breathless with laughter.

Another game was to swoop past me with a thought-splitting screech while I sat reading in the armchair. Just as I'd lift my head, startled, she would swoop back again, grazing my ear. Then she'd zoom past me repeatedly. My part was to clap my hands very suddenly just behind her tail as it blurred by as though she had just eluded capture. I often started this game too, by blocking the doorway when she was in the adjoining room, bouncing up and down clapping, and daring her to pass me. She could rarely resist joining in. If I was sitting in my chair with my hands up, poised to 'catch' her as she streaked towards me, she'd suddenly swoop past *under* the chair with incredible speed at the last possible moment and zoom off, a "ka-ka-ka" of derision floating back.

But the games were instantly stopped with a sudden sobering 'time out' when the eggs required warming. County's internal clock was infallible. When she was lured by hot sunny windowsills and lay indulging in a relaxing sun bath, I'd find myself getting more and more concerned about the eggs. Long after I was convinced she should be back on them, she'd still be sprawled, glassy-eyed and happy, in the sunshine. When I would finally check them myself, I'd find them perfectly warm and realize once again that she had the situation well in hand. Of course, with the non-fertile ones, there were no tiny lives at stake, but now I was hoping to find fertile ones, so the nesting procedure was crucial.

Bugs, meanwhile, was not only feeding himself with decreasing supervision, but was becoming more and more playful and venturesome. His first sight of Desmond and Molly was unforgettable, for both of us. Recalling how frightened Towne had been initially at their size, I decided to carry Bugs into the room where I'd isolated them behind a temporary screen door, and introduce him carefully. These particular domestic pigeons are at least twice the size of wild ones. I was afraid that if he spotted them suddenly on his own, he might panic and fly into window glass, hurting himself. I opened their door, and slowly glided towards the pigeons, cradling Bugs in my hands and murmuring reassuringly to him. The moment he saw them his eyes became absolutely enormous, his whole body grew rigid, and his entire bowel contents exploded copiously all down my front to my very knees. At that same moment there was a knock at the front door. The two of us made a memorable impression.

About a week after County began to lay, I arrived home one night about nine o'clock with four nestlings huddled in the remnants of their nest. Their tree had been felled by pulp cutters and they had been rescued by well-intentioned people who were puzzled as to how to care for them. Kindly attempts had been made to feed them raw egg, but they were still gaping hungrily with sticky faces and desperate cries. They were smaller than robin nestlings, yet similarly coloured, so I wondered if they too were thrushes. We eventually established that they were indeed Swainson's thrushes.

When I entered the living room County flew off her nest and

I stood close to it, holding the baby thrushes. She was evidently disturbed by their calls, and circled about the vicinity, barking. I waited a few moments, till she had settled down nearby, then hurriedly sneaked her eggs into my jacket pocket and slipped the nestlings into the nest. County flew to one of the cowhorns; then to the nest rim. She stood there eyeing them while I told her feelingly of their need for her care. The little creatures no sooner saw County alight than they gaped frantically with shrill cries. County remained very still while I earnestly described the urgency of their situation, and of her proven capability, watching me and the thrushes in turn with dark serious eyes. The exhausted babes meanwhile slowly dwindled down into the nest, gaping half-heartedly and calling sporadically. Then, as she had with Bugs, County gently let down her brooding feathers, stepped in, and nestled down cozily over them all, gentle contentment expressed in every feather.

I let them stabilize peacefully for several minutes before taking up a handful of wrigglies. Then I stood by enchanted, as County briskly fed four desperate strangers to sleepy repletion, and busily disposed of minute fecal sacs before snuggling back down onto them, overflowing the nest and dissolving their anxieties with reassuring warmth for the rest of the night.

BEING catapulted suddenly into mothering four ever-hungry babies meant busy days for County. She was continually on the go from dawn to dusk—feeding, removing fecal sacs, warming, cleaning their sticky feathers, aerating the nest, gathering food, defending her territory—plus attending her own personal needs. She had no attention to spare for Bugs. Occasionally he'd still beg her to feed him, especially if she were in the bug box anyway, but got chased and trounced for his efforts. So he turned to me more frequently for food as well as feeding himself—even tweaking my nose early one morning at feeding time when I was still asleep in bed. But the new babies completely fascinated him, and he spent a lot of time with them, napping beside the nest when County warmed them or, even more marvellous, settling himself over them as carefully as any mother and warming them too. He was always gentle.

The young thrushes thrived happily under County's intensive care. When she'd arrive with food, all four necks would shoot straight up and all four mouths cry enthusiastically and shrilly to be fed. This seemed a clear indication that there were no weaklings needing special treatment—a relief to me, since I, too, had very little time to spare.

I was astounded at the quantities of insects necessary now each day with *six* mouths to feed. My waking thoughts, and dreams, were obsessed with ploys to ensnare yet more of the elusive wrigglies. Day by day, my respect for other foraging parents deepened to awe. The moths caught overnight in the porch barely held out till I got back at 8 a.m. with the first bucket load—three inches deep with crawling, writhing savouries. For me, dewy summer mornings meant being driven to distraction by mosquitos and flies for two intense hours while pawing through malodourous compost. By mid-afternoon another trip was essential, and even a third before nightfall—each time to a different spot. As the wild supply dwindled more each day, I tried rotating my hunting areas among the compost, the wood-splitting area, the stacked-wood area, the scattered-boards spot, and the rotting logs in the woods, so that I wouldn't comb the same place two days in a row. Wherever I sought insects, too, had to be free of possible chemical contamination. I even drove to the homes of friends—not to visit, but to forage with manic concentration through their yards and composts. At this rate, visiting was out of the question till Christmas at the earliest.

As wild strawberries, raspberries, chokecherries, and blueberries ripened, I'd add them to my supplies but they never seemed to possess the charisma of the wrigglies. The more rare or the more difficult to catch, the more desirable. And County was adamant that there be a decent *variety* of food, as well. If I managed to retrieve only earthworms (not so rare, and easy to catch), she'd root through the bug box tossing them aside till she'd made certain there was nothing else. Then she'd bounce out and stare balefully at me, every feather bristling indignantly. There was nothing for it but to don all the bug-resistant gear again and head out. I began to wonder in my less lucid moments if I had always spent my summers this way, or whether there had ever been a time when I *didn't* think only of insects. I positively embraced visitors arriving with fresh wriggling contributions—if anyone had brought me roses, I'd have cried.

Two or three days after they'd arrived, the baby thrushes were eagerly climbing out of the nest onto the cowhorns and up through the surrounding spruce branches. They were all fluffy by now from County's cleaning, and they hopped happily over the floors in every direction, their short half-inch tails giving them a stubby irresistible charm. Even with careful supervision, their days were riddled with adventures on a sliding scale of urgency. An hour or more of anxious searching would finally locate one speechless culprit corralled under the electric stove, an area he could only have reached from the rear, and a second trapped behind an upright box in quite another part of the house, silently awaiting rescue. In situations like these, they seemed so totally averse to announcing their dilemmas with a helpful 'location' note that I found myself wishing fervently for a divine bestowal of infra-red vision.

Bugs took great delight in swooping them, as County had been wont to do to him to encourage independence, but his enthusiasm frequently bowled them over. He was so much bigger than even County by now, and sporting the longest legs as well, that it was rather like watching a zesty colt frisking with chicks. It was probably excellent training for life in the wild, teaching them watchfulness in all directions; it also seemed an excessive method of instruction. But judgments on these sorts of matters I left entirely to County.

The thrushes tired easily in these early days, just as Bugs had done, and two would often lean cozily against each other, holding one another up as they watched the activities around them. Or they'd huddle down in heaps to doze under a warming lamp, or line themselves along a lampshade. County was in her element, carrying food all over the house to wherever the babes happened to be—and I was in another kind of element, following behind and cleaning up. Even Bugs lent a hand with the feedings but his good intentions outshone his abilities—he always crouched before the thrushes, edging the food out straight towards them while they persisted in gaping upward futilely, fixing a sidelong bewildered eye on him at the same time.

By now, I had realized the inadequacy of the first garden and, with boards and sheets of plastic, had enlarged it to an eight-by-ten-foot capacity which met with everyone's approval. Between foraging trips and after counting beaks, I would ease back in my chair and simply enjoy all the comings and goings throughout the greenery. The thrushes were everywhere at once (I was convinced there were more than four)—in and out of the bug box, splashing through the waterdishes, playing "pounce" from behind the plant pots, chasing after County, and scuttling under the foliage whenever they saw Bugs swoop.

Then, when rain pattered on the roof and the dripping of water rang melodiously through the porch doorway, the garden would begin to harmonize with unfolding blossoms of song as all the birds began to sing.

CHAPTER EIGHT

BEDLAM

OF COURSE, WITH THE THRUSHES OUT OF THE NEST AND MOBILE, and Bugs and County constantly on the go, our borderline lifestyle deteriorated rapidly into unprecendented chaos. I was only mildly surprised one day when I passed a toad in the dining room. It hardly seemed out of place in a house where one was daily picking up unwanted slugs or earthworms oozing stickily across the floors. And now with crash landings everywhere as the babies struggled with the mysteries of flight, household hazards increased proportionally—the tinier size of the thrushes render-ing them more vulnerable. How well I remember watching one little adventurer launch himself with admirable resolve from a lampshade and flutter steadily over the length of the garden, past the woodstove, and straight into the kitchen—only to collapse as suddenly as an expended balloon, straight down into the sole object on the counter—a mug half-full of cold tea. Simultaneously, another sprawled intricately in a bouquet of dried Chinese lanterns, his legs and wings presenting themselves at angles to his body that defied anatomical accuracy.

They would make concerted efforts to alight on a single leaf, or on a slender arching palm 'branch', only to be tipped off grace-fully into the water dish with a surprised splash. Their legs were so much shorter than the robins' that I didn't dare leave water more than an inch deep. They could also be defeated entirely by an empty bowl—lacking enough strength yet to lift out by wing-power, they would scramble endlessly up the sides until I scooped them out in passing. I resorted to covering my tea between sips, not knowing who (or what) might drop into it, and refused even to consider a bowl of hot soup till the family was grown. Tangling themselves in the hanging philodendron, getting lost in cupboards, losing the rest of the world in dark closets and persis-tently underfoot everywhere, the baby thrushes encountered each day's disasters with charm and oblivious innocence. Bugs added to their habitual confusion by unexpectedly swooping and thumping them as they flew, his cockiness not a whit diminished by my indignant remonstrances. I would mutter darkly that his unquenchable devilishness was a direct inheritance from his mother's side of the family.

Besides providing natural recreation, the garden also served as an invaluable training ground for adult bird life in the wild. Now that Bugs was picking up things, (even trying to pick up red spots printed in a catalogue and ignoring the other colours), I would try to present his food in as natural a way as possible. This meant surreptitiously burying a bug, luring him over and in simulated astonishment prodding the bug out of the earth as though my finger were a beak. Then I'd push it about a little, while Bugs watched in fascination. Finally, I'd flick it towards him in hopes that he would dispose of it, which he usually did. He made the analogy between finger and beak very quickly, and we often prodded bugs together as happily as any other father and son.

By now he too was bathing regularly in the water dish, and County soon delivered the same ultimatum to Bugs as to Towne, driving him away so she could bathe in privacy. Fortunately for her peace of mind, Bugs didn't resort to skulking through the shrubbery to tease her, as Towne had done. But he quickly came up with a rejoinder. Just as County would chase and trounce him to make her meaning clear, so Bugs would choose a moment when County was airborne, swoop down from above and thump her to the ground with obvious glee.

Nevertheless, County's enthusiasm for motherhood was unflagging. Even a rare treat, like the huge spiders she adored, she would pound properly, savour longingly, and then ram resolutely into a hungry throat. Not content with feeding the four thrushes all day and everywhere, she began once more to make preparations for a *third* family. Like other fathers in similar situations, I turned a deaf ear, even creeping out of the house one night with the empty nest and cow skull and hiding it in the woodshed to discourage her. But County was adamant. I thought back to the day she chose to stay—and returned the skull to the living room. County immediately built a new nest and we again shared our courtship.

Her high spirits were boundless. Spotting a big horsefly in the house one morning, she flashed about at high speed with great dexterity, stopping suddenly with it clutched triumphantly in her beak, her eyes dancing. I was so delighted for her, beaming my congratulations across the room, that she swooped over to me, and placed it for a moment in my mouth as to one of her own babes.

It was a very special gesture. It was also a very difficult moment for a human and a vegetarian.

THE BABY thrushes were now coming more under my jurisdiction for feedings—as had happened with Bugs. I had established quite a special rapport with one of them whose left leg may have been dislocated when their original nest was felled. The leg remained at an unnatural angle, but he was one of the first out of the nest. As I'd stand on the couch gazing in at the little creatures, he'd hop from the rim onto one of the horns. From there, he'd sway back and forth in an undecided manner, peering for another perch to conquer. So I'd obligingly present my finger a few inches beyond the horn. Eyeing it eagerly, he'd patter his feet a few times, gather himself mightily, and leap—with a squeak of triumph on landing. Then I'd move my hand backward, with him gripping tightly, until the cowhorn was ahead of him, and he'd ready himself for another big leap—all of six inches. Again he'd peep, looking excitedly at me. Once more I'd put my finger beyond the horn and we'd do it again and again, both of us enjoying ourselves wonderfully.

Feeding the thrushes was easier in the beginning, because unlike Bugs, they gaped readily. Before long, they (as well as Bugs) were flocking around me begging to be fed whenever I'd arrive with a fresh load of wrigglies. I had begun to eliminate the occasional gigantic earthworm from my gleanings after seeing how long County needed to pound the creatures in order to render them fit to eat. Quite frankly, I couldn't bear it—and also I worried about the thrushes choking on worms so huge being pushed into their throats which were smaller than those of robins. One memorable instance saw each end of an oversize worm thrust solidly into two throats simultaneously, neither throat attempting to swallow or eject it. The worm had been so battered in its 'preparation' as food that its life was nearly terminated. Loath to let it linger indefinitely, and feeling personally responsible for its dilemma, I resolutely forced myself to cut it into three pieces with scissors. Then I quickly pushed the sections into three receptive throats. It was the most merciful thing to do. But I do wish the memory would fade.

Mealworms, on the other hand, were far easier for all of us, and were prime favourites with everyone as well, being forever snatched away in wily raids. County being unquestionably at the top of the pecking order, I would feed her several first, also hoping that then she'd be less inclined to take anyone else's. Then Bugs and I would share another prodding and catching lesson in the garden. Finally, I would gather the little thrushes together and drop a few mealworms in their midst. Great interest would immediately be aroused, and they'd collect in a little circle around the worms, fascinated. Then I'd gently prod the mealies for a little while, before picking one up and holding it before the round eyes of the thrushes who would instantly cry and gape to be fed, beating their wings frantically. So I'd place it just inside one beak, but not down into the throat, so that the mandibles would grip the worm when they closed together. Invariably the thrush would just stand there, seemingly surprised and undecided, before either swallowing or dropping it. I'd persist in maintaining their interest by prodding and picking up the mealworms, using just my thumb and index finger, and tucking the other fingers under so that my hand would look as beaklike as possible.

Eventually the thrushes began to participate too—but more as though engaged in a mysterious ritual from the mists of antiquity. Standing silently in their little circle, garbed in the ancient infancy of nestlings, they'd stare down as though spellbound at the mealworms in their centre. Then one would reach hesitantly towards them, only to draw back again, and so would another, and perhaps another. Then the boldest would break the sequence and actually seize a mealworm, holding it while the others eyed him silently. If he neither dropped nor swallowed it, another thrush would reach across and solemnly take it away. Then he, too, would stand there holding the worm. If he neither dropped nor swallowed it, it would be carefully taken either by the former thrush or by another. If the worm were dropped, all the thrushes would resume staring at it silently, still in their circle. But if one actually swallowed it, three pairs of eyes would be fastened on him for several moments, before being transferred down to the remaining mealworms in the centre.

Crass outsider that I was, my mirth would soon get the better of me, and I would beat a hasty retreat to a more profane atmosphere where I could laugh long and uproariously, disrupting no one.

UPS AND DOWNS

OUR ENTWINING LIVES BEGAN TO SUFFER AT THIS POINT FROM catastrophes and increasing tension. Another robin fledgling about Bugs's age slammed into one of our windows at high speed. I have small silhouettes of hawks painted on the outside of all the windows to discourage the illusion of reflected sky, but although this diminishes the problem, it doesn't eradicate it. Casualties may occur several times in a summer, or not at all, but strangely enough, it doesn't happen in winter. Usually I pick up the stunned bird as quickly as possible because of predators, and sit down immediately in silence, holding him covered by my hands—closely enough to provide security and dimness, loosely enough not to overheat. Anywhere from half-an-hour to an hour-and-a-half is necessary for recovery. Gradually the rapid breathing slows to normal and is followed by sleep. When the toes begin to grip, I can feel fairly certain he'll recover. When little restless movements follow, I open my hands a little and speak calmly and quietly. Soon I'll feel that it's time to place him gently on a branch and back slowly away, speaking softly and conveying whatever reassurance I can. Very rarely does one not recover and eventually fly away.

One of the most beautiful birds I ever helped in this way was a male ruby-throated hummingbird. He sat for quite a while in my hands after he had recovered, watching me without fear, and the coming and going of the sun in the clouds found an echoing pulse in the glowing and fading of his incredible iridescent plumage. Another delightful bird was a pine siskin, his curiosity aroused, who began climbing fearlessly up my arm to my shoulder after he'd recovered.

I followed my established procedure with the young robin, noting before I released him that his eyes were deep and bright, and his toes gripped well. But when he tried to fly, he nose-dived straight into the ground. Appalled, I picked him up again, thinking that perhaps a little longer rest was needed. In case my presence would frighten him now that he was conscious, I sat beside the indoor garden holding him where he could watch birds who didn't fear me—and this indeed steadied him. He sat quietly nestled in my hands so interested in the others that he rarely even glanced at me. After another hour or so, I tried once more to launch him—but again he plummeted to the ground. His wings felt normal and beat well, so I suspected some sort of brain or nerve damage; hopefully, temporary. Finally I set him in a box on a shelf overlooking the indoor garden, restraining his movements with screening across the front of it. I hoped that a night's rest would restore his flying control, but the next morning saw no change, although in appearance he looked perfectly normal. So I rubbed rotenone powder (for parasites) throughout his feathers and released him into the family garden. I had already inflicted the same organic powder on the rest of the birds as a precautionary measure, only Bugs holding an indignant grudge still. So 'Bang,' as I called him, joined the family.

At first all went well. Bugs and the thrushes had no objections to Bang's arrival, although they were frequently startled upon confronting him as he lurked nervously in the shrubbery. And County was engrossed in her new eggs. The day before Bang hit the window, about two weeks after the arrival of the thrushes, County laid the first egg of her third clutch. Two more eggs followed during the next two days, and the time of Bang's inclusion in the family circle saw her happily brooding three sound eggs. I, meanwhile, was spending nearly all day, every day, hunting for insects, most of my bug sources drying up in the mid-July heat. I was constantly preoccupied with the problem of food for the birds; finding enough for *seven* was extremely worrisome.

At this point, one of the thrushes, unobserved, entered the room at the opposite end of the house where Desmond and Molly were still restricted from County's nesting territory, the door unfortunately being ajar. The sight of two huge (to him) pigeons must have panicked him and I heard another loud bang

County joyfully anticipating mother-hood (above).

She always had absolute trust in me handling her babe—the arrival of Bugs (right).

Facing page:
Just as she had known exactly how to build a nest, County knew exactly how to care for her young.

County and Bugs (top).

Over the next few days, Bugs grew like an inflating balloon (right).

Bugs about two weeks old. Tail feathers are the last to lengthen, there being no room, or need, for them in the nest.

Bugs, in a very unusual photograph, broods the Swainson Thrush nestlings (above), while County indulges in a relaxing sunbath (right).

Soon the baby thrushes were eagerly climbing out of the nest (left) and County carried food to them all over the house (below).

Devilish Bugs looking for mischief (above).

I established a special rapport with one of the thrushes (right).

County always appreciated a cool drink as she rested after laying an egg (above).

Facing page:
When Burp was born, she was the tiniest robin nestling I'd ever seen—about the size of a large gumdrop (top left). At one week old, her ear is still visible below her eye (top right). At ten days, her baby down is still attached to the tips of her new juvenile plumage (right).

Burp glorying in a sunbath and drinking in the heat.

Squeek gaped for food immediately after hatching (above). At four days old, Squeek was much larger than the eggs. The upward-facing vent is clearly visible, as the tail has not yet begun to protrude (right).

When Squeek would gape for food, Burp would inexplicably seize his beak in a gentle but firm grip causing great consternation (top).

Burp at five weeks of age, just prior to her successful launching into the wild (above left and right).

on the window. I held the little thrush as I had held Bang, trying to calm and reassure him, and he gradually recovered—but his coordination was unhappily affected.

To increase our difficulties, County began zooming off her nest whenever she spotted Bang in the open, and pounding him vehemently. Bang never attempted to defend himself, so several times I broke up very serious tussles in which County was unquestionably trying to rid him from her territory altogether. When I'd pull her off him, she'd glare speakingly at me before returning to her nest. Obviously I wasn't fulfilling my defense duties, as expected of a spouse. I began to wonder if Bang would have to go for his *own* sake. I also wondered where.

Then, two days after hitting the window, the little thrush was found lying dead in the garden. I felt acutely how remiss I had been in the vigilance required to protect him, and how unnecessary was his death. With great sadness I laid him beneath the birch tree near Towne.

Bugs meanwhile was really beginning to harass the other thrushes with his roughhousing, although it was quite obviously carried out in fun. The same could not be said of County, who was still attacking Bang at every opportunity while he scuttled as unobtrusively as possible between the garden and the adjacent screened porch. He was unable to get up on the table out there, but as soon as he watched me set up a 'ladder' of small boxes for him, he immediately hopped up and sat leaning against the screen, gazing out longingly. I couldn't approach him without frightening him but I frequently tossed him worms and bugs, without looking directly at him, which he'd gobble eagerly. But whenever County caught sight of him, she invariably shot after him. I could stop her if I was close at hand, but the situation was a terrible burden—especially when I was out so often hunting for food for everyone. In desperation, I spoke to a wildlife biologist friend who came up with the only solution possible at the time. He took Bang, comfortably ensconced in a budgie cage and eating a liberal supply of chokecherries, in his car to a wildlife park with a large, varied bird population and released him. There would be a constant supply of natural and scattered food throughout dense foliage so that he could provide for himself. Neither of us could know if his flying control would ever return to normal, but it seemed the only possible answer under the circumstances. A caged life was never even considered.

THE REMAINING three thrushes, in the meantime, were learning day by day to catch and eat their own food. Gradually, the mealworm ritual gave way to brisk efficient gobblings—with competitive stimulation from Bugs and County. In the porch, they too began to catch moths, missing more than they caught, but increasing noticeably in skill each morning. Sowbugs, though, were their specialty—fast enough to be interesting, slow enough to be caught. At this stage, I began to restrain myself from feeding or handling the thrushes except on rare occasions, hoping in this way to stimulate more independence and self-sufficiency. I kept the food box supplied as well as possible with bugs covered with a few inches of dirt to encourage hunting, but faded more into the background of their lives. A certain wariness around other humans began to be noticeable with them now, as well as with Bugs, and this I also wished to foster. When they were ready to be released, I didn't want to limit their chances with an unreserved trust in humans.

Bugs I had finally restricted to the same room as the pigeons. He was in so little awe of them now as to chase them whenever they flew, although he never attempted to thump them down to the floor, and they weren't in the least troubled by him. I set up a small apple tree there for him, as well as a little garden well seeded with bugs. I had found his aerial attacks on County and the thrushes too distressing to ignore any longer.

Initially, I had hoped to keep Bugs with us permanently as a robin companion for County, Towne being gone. But I was learning how wrong I had been to consider this. County, held back originally because of health reasons, was a house robin now of her own free choice. Towne, held back as well for health reasons, had never shown the least inclination to venture outside into the world that caused her so much fear. But Bugs was a large, full-spirited robin in perfect health—by spring the house would be far too small for him.

Meanwhile, no sooner had I removed Bugs from the immediate vicinity of the thrushes than County began to chase them, swooping off her nest to do so. I saw that the time had come, as it does in the wild, when one family of siblings has to disperse to make room for the next. But the thrushes, in only three-and-a-half weeks, had evolved from tufty, eager-eyed nestlings to birds capable of feeding themselves; alert, quick of movement (thanks to Bugs), and amazingly adult now in their appearance. I released them a short distance from the house in hilly mixed forest and beside a stream—I was particularly concerned that water be instantly available, since in their training I had been unable to avoid the unnatural appearance of waterdishes. We all sat silently watching each other for a while, the thrushes perched in a big spruce overhanging the brook, myself kneeling on the ground. Then I turned away and left them.

A little over a year later, I heard unusual and excited sounds from County. Joining her at the windowsill, I saw an adult Swainson's Thrush up on the porch roof watching her, but he fluttered away at sight of me. For at least a week after that, I saw one—or perhaps more than one—outside the various windows of the house and I had never noticed Swainson's Thrushes near the house before. They have a tremendously-long migratory path to South America and the intervening hazards are appallingly high, but County's unusual excitement was enough to convince me of the indentity of our rare little visitor.

A WEEK after the laying of her third egg, County, to my immense relief, stopped brooding. There was no doubt that we were both exhausted, and I fancied, too, that she was thinner. I never saw her resting and sleeping so continuously as I did throughout the following weeks, when she was also moulting. I was feeling decidedly numb myself. But Bugs, free to join us once more, was still buoyant and mischievous, and now resumed his aerial attacks on County whenever he saw her flying. As a result, she began to spend whole days silently hiding under the plants, where even then Bugs would try to provoke her, regardless of my weary protests. After one particularly rough encounter between them, County looked earnestly and speakingly at me, and I knew he had to go.

Early the next morning, while County was still asleep in the bathroom on the shower rod, I gently closed her door and opened the door into the screen porch. Bugs, up early and ready for fun, joined me, pulling chokecherries off the branches kept available out there in jugs of water. I closed the door leading back into the house. Then I sat with him for awhile. He had always been a fun companion to me, and releasing him wasn't going to be easy. But County and I had a very special commitment to each other—and a prior one. And I knew that Bugs would eventually find the house unhappily confining. So finally, I opened the outside door, stepped out, and called to Bugs. After a few moments, he flew onto my head but, startled at seeing sky above him instead of a ceiling, he flew back in. Then, after a pause, he flew back to my head and cast up a chokecherry pit. After a few excited flicks, he flitted up onto the porch roof. At that moment, a flock of juvenile robins that I had often noticed around the house, swooped past overhead. Bugs instantly darted after them, 'chasing' no doubt, and they all passed over the roof out of sight. He was big, strong, capable and distrustful now of other humans. And he would learn more from the wild juveniles. I had wonderful confidence in him...but I never, to my knowledge, saw him again.

Half an hour later, I went to the closed, windowless bathroom to let County out and to tell her that Bugs would no longer harass her. She already knew! She was crouched in the dark on the rod ready to spring, all her feathers sticking out in her most excited playful manner—the one she used when I approached with a palmful of mealworms—and her eyes shining brightly. With a whoop she shot out past me and soared freely back and forth from one end of the house to the other, upstairs and downstairs, and round and around again as I hadn't seen her do since Bugs was newly out of the nest. I found myself pulled painfully between opposite feelings—deep sadness at losing Bugs, and deep happiness at regaining the high-spirited County I had always known.

I realized, on reflection, that circumstances had only become intensely problematic whenever I failed to deal with each unfolding phase as would a male robin spouse—that is, without questioning those duties which, as an erring, though well-intentioned, human I had only partially, although to the best of my abilities, fulfilled.

CHAPTER 10
WINTER GAMES

THROUGHOUT THE MONTHS THAT FOLLOWED our first nesting season, County and I fell back into our usual mode of quieter enjoyments. But I felt we were even closer after sharing courtship and parenthood. My offering tidbits to her seemed to have a deeper significance, as though the gesture in itself had gained an importance quite apart from the particular food in question. Her wild games, offsetting the intensity of her brooding periods, gave way to lighter diversions like chasing mice out of the garden or bouncing off the top of my head after being fed—not to forget flying off devilishly with a piece of chalk I was using, only to be waiting for me with all feathers raised in high amusement upstairs beside the mealworms as I arrived, panting. And then there was the Great Mealworm Caper.

Whenever I had to leave the house for a prolonged time, I tried to leave two or three small dishes of mealworms in bran, strategically spaced throughout the house to allow her to discover them gradually. Thus, she was unable to gobble them all in the first hour, leaving her hungry until I returned. Soon her joy in anticipating feasts of mealworms replaced her solemn-eyed expression whenever she realized my impending absence, and successfully hiding the dishes rapidly evolved into a hilarious free-for-all. My preparations for leaving—switching off music and extraneous lighting, changing my clothes, adjusting the wood stove—would all tip her off, and she'd immediately begin to monitor my movements. At this point, I would feign reading or a little house cleaning until she lost interest and drifted away. Then I would tiptoe quietly upstairs to the aquarium with the utmost stealth, where I would hastily gather mealworms into the dishes. Setting the lid back on noiselessly with excruciating precision, and turning carefully around, I would suddenly laugh aloud; there she'd be, sitting directly behind me on the bedpost in silence, watching with obvious, suppressed mirth.

Then she'd zip up onto my head and pull my hair, her special signal for wanting a mealworm. Diverting her by dropping a couple on the bed, I would scuttle at full speed down the stairs to hide a dish in the garden, only to find awaiting me the same robin I thought I'd left upstairs. Had she not still been swallowing I might have thought there were two of them. So I'd spin around, dash partway upstairs, double back and bolt into the dining room, hastily pushing a dish amongst protruding plant leaves on the table just as County, thinking to foil me by swooping up to the loft from the garden, but finding herself foiled instead, would hurtle down the stairwell in hot pursuit. In a blur, she'd pass over my head as I'd duck and spin around back to the garden, only to be greeted by a bristling ball of animated feathers, a pair of eyes dancing with merriment, and a cocky bark of triumph. Were there *three* robins?

Another of our 'winter games' was hide-and-seek, which often got under way when I called to County that I had a treat for her. Hearing a single answering chirp, which I thought came from the other end of the house, I'd roam off in that direction searching for her. Looking around in vain, I would call again, and again would hear a single chirp. This time I was certain it was coming from the loft, and wondering how I could possibly have mistaken the location, I'd climb the stairs and find no one. Then I'd hear a single chirp again—it must have come from the back porch all this time. But just as I'd arrive there, I'd hear it again well behind me. Convinced by now she was teasing me and determined to outwit her, I'd start sneaking through the house, room by room, in perfect silence, peering into every nook and cranny—only to hear one more mind breaking chirp coming from the areas I'd just combed. Wheeling around, I'd stealthily retrace my route step by step only to be startled by a sudden whirr by my ear as she thumped down on my shoulder from behind me, pulling my hair in devilish delight to get her treat. I preferred to consider a defect in my hearing, rather than question my comparative intelligence.

Her nightly roost, once again, was on the shower rod, and it gradually evolved that we regularly spent the last hour of daylight in each other's company in the adjoining room which also housed the pigeons. It had a comfortable lounge chair in which I'd recline with County close to me, as we all watched in silence the day's fading. When it was time to roost, she'd swoop out of the room into the dark bathroom and up onto the shower rod. This heralded another game. Without a sound, she'd suddenly zoom back out of the bathroom straight at my face, swerving at the last possible fraction of a second to thump onto the top of my head, or sheer off to land beside me. All my resolution failed to prevent me from flinching slightly and shutting my eyes as she all but brushed my face at high speed—a triumph for her. She might do it several times or only once; keeping me in suspense as to when or whether she'd suddenly appear out of the darkness was half the fun, I'm sure. But I would no sooner begin to rise, assuming she was finally roosted, when with a squeak she'd swoop me again and I'd duck, losing the game beyond question.

Although during the nesting season, County tended her babies regardless of occasional human visitors, sometimes obviously quelling her natural nervousness, during the rest of the year she rarely showed herself to strangers. Her anxiety around humans was particularly acute just before her spring 'migrating' as her energies were rising, when she would hide in the upstairs closet should anyone stop in. Thus, her roosting all winter in the bathroom meant that any evening visitors who needed to relieve themselves had to resort to chilling outdoor facilities to avoid frightening County—truly a test of friendship. One evening in early autumn I was expecting six people for a dinner-meeting, an unusually large number for me. They were due to arrive before County would normally be at rest, and I worried for days about coaxing her to roost ahead of her time, to avoid the fright several strangers would inadvertently give her. Visions of her panicking and flying into the windows haunted me, but she had the situation well in hand. On her own initiative, and at least forty minutes before they were due, County hopped onto the top of the protruding bathroom door as I happened to approach, looked at me knowingly and flew in to roost. I stopped to speak softly to her as she settled herself, and then gently closed the door. The only other times she volunteered to roost early, I was again expecting people for dinner. She never ceased to amaze me.

ONE FALL day I was offered a wild pigeon with a damaged bill, who had been sheltered by some kind-hearted people. The tip of one mandible was broken off, and unless seed was kept available in a deep dish, "Walter" couldn't eat. He was unable to pick up single seeds on the ground. The people couldn't keep him indefinitely, and releasing him didn't seem possible, because beak injuries don't return to normal. He was quiet, gentle, and cooperative, like each wild pigeon I've known, and I was interested in integrating him into our family. But I felt that the birds themselves should decide. And Walter's humans agreed.

I built a couple of shelves in the room Desmond and Molly occupied, and set out dishes of food and water on them. Then I brought in Walter, housed for transport in a large budgie cage. Although she wasn't near at the time, I anticipated no objections from County, since she'd been accustomed to pigeons all her life; rather, I felt the issue rested with Desmond and Molly. As soon as I set Walter on his shelf, great interest sprang up among the three, and they all regarded each other with rapt fascination. Happily, there was no feeling of animosity to mar the situation, and my hopes mounted, since I'd already grown fond of Walter. When nearly an hour had passed without County meeting him, I called her into the room, mealworms in my hand.

No sooner did she catch sight of him than her eyes widened enormously and she instantly vanished. I was utterly astounded. Hunting everywhere, I finally discovered her hiding and trembling in the upstairs closet. No amount of coaxing would lure

her out. She was securely entrenched, and her eyes were still terrified. When I whispered calmingly of Walter's gentleness and
offered a finger-perch, she lowered her head defensively and
opened her bill at me. As on previous occasions, I remembered
the moving tribute of her decision to stay with me. The
premises were as much hers as mine after everything we'd
shared. Although I would have enjoyed welcoming Walter to
our circle, I couldn't even consider forcing County against such
fear. And I wasn't able to understand the cause of her fear; never
in our years together had I seen her this frightened. Regretfully,
I gathered up mild, unprotesting Walter, replaced him in his
travelling cage, and set him again in the truck, ready to be
returned. Back at the closet, I apologized to County, explained
very earnestly that Walter was no longer in the house, and asked
her to come with me to see for herself. Then I again offered a
finger-perch. After a short hesitation, she stepped on, and I
slowly and carefully carried her downstairs and out to the
pigeons' area, speaking reassuringly all the while. She allowed
herself to be carried the whole distance, a most unusual conces-
sion with her, but gripped my finger more and more tightly as
we came to Walter's shelves. After a few moments there, I carried her through the rest of the downstairs, arriving again at
Walter's shelves to ease her fears completely. Reassured entirely,
she quickly relaxed and swooped off my hand to a window-
perch, all her fears dissolving, and her whole being radiating
relief and happiness. Then she bustled off for a drink of water
before resuming her usual activities, while I drove Walter back
to his humans with considerable perplexity.

What could it have been that County feared in Walter?
What did she know, by means other than those we understand?
She had seen me hold several other wild birds recovering from
window-crashes or rescued from roadways; never had she shown
such fright. But I've had inexplicable experiences myself on very
rare occasions, when near a human I didn't know and yet intu-
itively feared. Most of us have experienced sudden, instinctive

dislikings. As we drove away, Walter and I glanced frequently at each other, and I had no idea which of us was more puzzled, or which of us had greater reason to be so.

Eventually, a vet trimmed the longer of Walter's two mandibles so that they matched exactly, enabling him finally to pick up single seeds and yet still preen. He was later released successfully, among wild pigeons in the same area where he'd previously been rescued.

Besides pondering County's reaction, I often wondered what Desmond and Molly thought about a strange pigeon being set before them for a viewing and then suddenly removed—to say nothing of Walter's thoughts. For them, the ever-inscrutable activities of humans must be constantly entertaining.

ANOTHER of County's wholly-unpredictable reactions occurred when a person of only slight acquaintance visited for the first time. He was a small, frail, chronically-unwell man of exceedingly gentle demeanor, who was suffering at the time from a persistent strain of mild influenza. In spite of his ill health he radiated cheerfulness and a bright spirit, speaking enthusiastically on various topics. As his visit concurred with County's shyest time of the year, I was highly surprised to see her being unusually tolerant of his presence—not to mention her being visible at all. As our visit lengthened, I was positively astonished to see her deliberately edge nearer to him, and then actually perch directly in front of him, only a couple of feet away. He glanced at her from time to time as he chatted, while I tried to reduce my eyes to their normal size and keep my attention on what he was saying. When County actually yawned, and began preening unconcernedly, I concluded that I was dreaming. The visitor himself, of course, had no idea that he was breaking all previous records. Perhaps he assumed that I usually listened with my eyes bulging to their utmost.

As THE winter months slipped by, I especially enjoyed studying the easily-overlooked subtleties in County that few others were as fortunate to see. Her facial expressions fascinated me—how did she convey them? Suddenly, depending perhaps on a flex of feathers, or a shaping to her eye, she would strongly resemble Towne, sometimes even Bugs. And although Towne, Bugs and County were all robins, they didn't in the least look alike. For myself, I've frequently confused humans who didn't at all resemble each other, but whose facial expressions were similar.

Nor were County's eyes, seen in close proximity, so relentlessly rounded as is often portrayed by artists striving for naturalism. Fear would round them to that degree, but throughout her daily activities her eyes were everchanging in shape and expression. I would be hard-pressed to describe just how she expressed humour, for instance, with her eyes—or how anyone does with unmoving facial muscles. But humour she did convey, and frequently at my expense.

Her emotional expressiveness was most interesting when County 'read the newspaper' in the little protruding greenhouse window. From this vantage point she could see to either side, as well as above and straight ahead. Cocking an eye over her shoulder, she could also see out the windows on the opposite wall. Perching there in the sunshine, totally absorbed, she'd catch up on all the happenings, her crest feathers continually flexing, her eyes varying constantly in shape and expression. Her entire body would react—a twitch, a fluffing or flattening of feathers, a huddling-down in defense, a stretching-upwards to full height as she peered curiously, a tightening grip, a yawn. Her own capability for perfect stillness between reactions would allow her to detect the slightest movement elsewhere. For me, it was all a closed book—I might well see the raven pass overhead, causing her to crouch in response, but the origins of the myriad reactions involving her entire presence were totally hidden from me. Given all her senses for only a few moments would provide me with a revelation of the natural world beyond my imaginings, a living drama of which I only ever see the undrawn curtain.

Reflections in water intrigued her too, although mirrors had no appeal. As a prelude to bathing, she would invariably crouch forward like a diver on the rim of the dish, her beak hovering low over the water, and peer into the mysterious looking-glass world below—the glassy surface transformed into the threshold of an unreachable yet familiar world, dissolvable at a touch.

THE PIGEONS on the other hand, enjoyed bathing untroubled by worlds within worlds. If I failed to offer them bathing water, they'd suggest it themselves by standing in their dry bath and looking pointedly at me. After filling it, I'd fill the plant mister too, because Desmond and Molly, unlike County, preferred a shower-bath. They'd refuse to share the water dish, but taking turns, they'd step in, soaking their beautifully feathered feet while I continually directed a steady spray all over them. Even the wild pigeons I've helped over the years loved a showerbath. Desmond and Molly would even lift one wing, holding it high on their backs while I sprayed their 'wing pits,' before lowering it and raising the other wing. Desmond, especially, loved to lie down in the water, his eyes closed blissfully, and simply bask in the constant rain beading up and cascading in little rivulets down over his feathers. Molly's delight, after her own session in the water, was to fly straight up out of the bath, spin completely around or fly backwards, and shake off the excess drops. Neither Desmond nor Molly beat their wings in the water like County, but leaning down, they'd shake their heads in a watery flurry that would produce a clean floor over a four-foot radius. County, meanwhile, enjoyed dabbling in the pools as they meandered in every direction, getting surprised by the occasional squirt of water when my diabolical nature emerged.

When Desmond and Molly were finally content, and their immediate surroundings satisfactorily saturated, they'd preen in a warm spot, their feathers squeaking like wet hair as they were pulled through their beaks. Desmond often liked to dry himself on top of my head (usually a suitable hotspot). It's rather surprising how heavy a large, wet pigeon can feel pressing down on one's head for half an hour—and how oddly statues come to mind.

ALTHOUGH County and I verbalized differently, in the shadowy realm beyond our differences we mingled our communications. It was an interesting weave; offerings were given and accepted from both sides, and that we could share a common language was fortunate indeed—especially at crucial times, as with Walter. And even at less crucial times.

One afternoon, when I was busily absorbed at one end of the house, County arrived from the direction of the kitchen clucking in alarm. I looked automatically out of the window, assuming that a cat was nearby, but all the wild birds were feeding calmly. County, though, was still uneasy, so I wandered, puzzled, out towards the kitchen. There I was met by a river of hot soup bubbling up from a forgotten pot, streaming down the sides of the stove, and oozing across the floor. Thanks to her, the situation didn't become any worse.

On another occasion, after a visitor with long hair had left, I noticed County tugging frequently at one foot. Examination revealed a long strand of hair wound tightly around and around her leg and toes, and tightening more in response to her efforts to rid herself of it. I made several attempts to grasp it, but she refused to allow me to handle her, and the hair progressively tightened. So finally, I stood back, conveying as clearly as I could that if she would just allow me to help, I would be able to free her very quickly; otherwise, the hair would injure her. Then I sat back down in my armchair to read. About five minutes later, County landed on the back of the chair. Turning my head, I understood that she was asking for help. So I carefully held her, unwound the strand as rapidly and gently as possible, and set her back down. It was the only situation in which I'd been forced to take hold of her that she didn't struggle indignantly.

MY PREOCCUPATION with insects throughout the summer months wasn't lessened by the end of the nesting season. Live food in mid-winter could be very difficult to obtain in satisfactory quantities, and County was adamant about live food—a personal viewpoint she made unquestionably clear. With cooler temperatures prevailing, reproduction and growth in the mealworm culture was slowed drastically; County's appetite, however, wasn't. Until I finally managed to order large numbers of mealworms by air through the kind efforts of an animal care technician, County was often forced to depend mostly on cheese and fruit for sustenance—a restriction she did not accept with grace. One solution, which eased the situation for about a month, was to collect hundreds of hibernating houseflies huddled in various nooks and crannies in the garage of friends. I stored the drowsy flies in airy paper bags laid flat in the fridge, to maintain their hibernation. Bottles of flies dropped off by friends living in those old farmhouses, which mysteriously produce flies at every thaw, joined the sleepers in the fridge. Then I would shake out two or three dozen into the garden each day—if possible, when County was elsewhere, giving the flies time to warm up and get mobile, providing her not only live food, but with exercise in pursuing them.

Another friend, arriving one day with much-needed mealworms, was hoping for a closer look at the elusive County. So I coaxed County near with an open palm covered with mealies, then transferred them to my friend's palm, raising County's 'eyebrows' quizzically. But standing calmly beside the visitor's hand and speaking reassuringly, I eventually persuaded her to land on it. My friend was thrilled. The wily County, too, was thrilled, at the prospect of a surfeit of mealworms that had meanwhile fanned out in tempting array. But as she snatched up one of the nearest, the sudden movement caused one at the edge to fall off. Cocking her head, she immediately sized up the problem and rapidly devoured all the mealworms around the edges to prevent any more escapees, before concentrating on the remainder in the middle. As a final flourish, she cornered the one on the floor.

LIVING closely on equal terms with birds not only develops one's ability to communicate, it broadens one's thinking beyond the habitual. I became humorously aware of this when an acquaintance of mine was holding forth about recent reports of strange UFOs filled with fearsome aliens. She exclaimed how terrified she'd be of meeting any—especially because of their alleged horrific appearance, an assumption common to Earthlings. Her dismay at the prospect of strangely-clad creatures with weirdly-shaped arms, and eyes on the sides of their heads tempted me to inform her wryly that I'd been living with creatures like that for years, and that they were, without doubt, beneficial to human existence.

CHAPTER ELEVEN
SPRING MIRACLE

THROUGHOUT THE MONTH OF MARCH, as her spring energies began to mobilize preceding her second nesting season, County again became high-strung, and utterly intolerant of other humans. Even my shaking out laundry or picking up a jacket near her would ignite in her a sudden alarm, forcing me to consider and constrain every action. But one morning, she snuggled close to my face, putting her beak into my mouth several times, her eyes dark with a special expression—a prelude, I felt, to courtship, and a delightful moment.

Beginning Easter Sunday in late March, just as I was marvelling at the rare appearance of a Varied Thrush at the feeder, County began 'migrating' and continued right into May. Day and night, her wild whistles and long swooping flights back and forth, up and down, filled the house. She slept whenever fatigue overcame her, sometimes spending part of each night nestled down drowsily on my head. As her energies thus became more channelled, her fears around other humans lessened, and I could relax more whenever friends stopped by. She also gathered hairs and threads daily from every conceivable spot, although without building, and sporadically practised the nest-building footwork in my hair when I was napping. Her appetite became voracious and her desire for fresh spring dirt to prod for bugs could only be described as manic. She had no interest in the male robins arriving daily from warmer climates, not even a rare one sporting white wings and back—a startling contrast with his brick-red breast. Our bond appeared to be inviolable—an immense relief to me.

She also engaged once again in a puzzling taste-testing of her own droppings, an action she reserved only for spring and fall, leading me to conjecture that she was checking on dietary deficiencies in connection with the arduous physical demands of migration. Often after tasting, she'd swallow some of the soft ash surrounding the woodstove—it seemed to be her only and automatic choice. Perhaps she was adjusting acidity.

Our courtship began again on the third of May, mingling for the next ten days with her constant flights the length of the house, frenetic gathering and intense indecision about the site of the new nest. Gradually she narrowed her choices down to the cowskull or a shelf above a door in a more secluded room, and she busily carried up mud and grasses to each in turn, testing them. The door won—and again, in one day of feverish activity, County built her nest. And once again, bog decor prevailed throughout the establishment, and footsteps tended to squish stickily when they didn't skid. I helped as before, in any way I could under her guidance, and persisted in offering her feedings, which she wolfed hastily—she would never stop long enough to eat otherwise. A contribution of mane and tail combings from a friend with horses gave County the perfect lining material to cradle the coming eggs. Knowing how easily long hairs entangle, I cut them into eight-inch lengths and scattered them over the garden where County gathered them happily, one by one. The lining was finished in less than a day. Now that she was completely prepared, County relaxed into high-spirited playfulness.

The following morning she endured an hour of laboured breathing in an aura of internal effort, with no egg. But she was so eager for motherhood that for the rest of the day she could *not* be pleased. Constantly restless, provoking the pigeons, tossing articles onto the floor, deliberately teasing me, demanding food but tossing it aside when it was offered, she roamed the house in a sulk, seeking distractions and leaving behind her a wake of distracted creatures. That night, rather than roosting, she slept on the old cowskull nest from the previous year, reminding me strangely of ancient fertility rites. But the next morning, after only five minutes of labour, she breathed the egg out safely into the new nest, and settled down over it happily, all petulance dissolved. Spring had come.

THREE more eggs arrived over the next three days, each a little later in the day than the previous one, and County was the happiest of robins, brooding steadily. Her infrequent swoops off the nest were again trumpeted loudly, and she'd dive at me devilishly, snapping her beak to start our wild chase games again as a foil to her long periods of inactivity. She'd be thrilled whenever I chased her around the chair legs under the diningroom table, snatching at her tail while she snapped at my fingers. If I wasn't available, she'd zoom through the pigeons' atmosphere of repose, swooping and provoking them, and scattering seed and chaos behind her as she swept off again. When she was hungry, she *demanded* food, and could barely restrain herself long enough to eat it. Then there'd be sudden silence and peace—County was back on her eggs.

Each time she came off the nest, I noticed that she'd land in a crouched position. Gradually she'd straighten as she bustled about, but I wondered if her legs became stiff or even temporarily weak after the intensive hours of brooding. If so, it was hardly surprising that she insisted on such wild exercise to counter-balance both the mental and physical constraints.

I, meanwhile, with County's hopes for motherhood constantly before me, was experiencing again the difficult, yet touching responsibility of being her spouse. Shortly after her last egg was laid, I began searching the woods for a nesting robin, and with happy results. By a stroke of luck, I spotted the pattern of undertail coverts in dense spruce foliage, and with the aid of a scope saw a female robin on a nest. Remaining hidden until she left the nest to feed, I cautiously removed one egg out of a clutch of three, setting it carefully into a well of cotton batting. Then I strode swiftly back to the house. County left her nest just as I came in, and I replaced two of her eggs with the wild one—to add more room when the little one was hatched. Then I checked on the wild robin again, and was relieved to see her brooding as usual. Back once more at the house, County, too, was brooding. All was well, and I poured a strong cup of tea while musing on the advantages of job-sharing to ease my twinges of conscience.

ONE morning five days later, County came zipping óut to me at the opposite end of the house barking excitedly and dropped a piece of blue eggshell. When I started up in surprise, she swept out of the room and back to her nest with me in hot pursuit. There, still struggling with the remainder of the shell, was the tiniest robin nestling I'd ever seen—about the size of a large gumdrop. She (as it later turned out) was still damp with a few straggles of down, had bulbous, sealed eyes, and the most incredibly tiny toes and wings. County stood on the edge of the nest, radiating happiness, her eyes glued to the miracle before her, while I watched too in reverence and awe. The eggshell was free now, and I carefully lifted it out. Then County stepped in and snuggled down over the babe, causing me to catch my breath in sudden anxiety—the little creature seemed so very small to be sat upon!

Forty-five minutes later, after several efforts, she gaped when County spoke and was fed. Within an hour or so, I could hear her chirping steadily underneath County as she brooded— another source of amazement. How on earth did the nestling breathe with County filling the nest? And wouldn't three or four nestlings cheeping at once betray the nest location in the wild? When feeding time came, I brought a tiny worm, and as County clucked the little one's beak open I carefully put in the worm. Never had I filled such a small beak; Bugs had been at least three times larger when he arrived. By evening, the nestling was gaping more strongly and seemed already larger than the egg from which she'd emerged only hours (and several feedings) ago.

The minute size and seeming fragility of the new arrival put me in a dither about gathering bugs for food—everything seemed chokingly huge for that tiny mouth. County, too, was limited in her choices to whatever I brought inside for her, and I pondered uneasily what she would choose if she were on her own. In the end, I tried to cover all possibilities. Besides the usual selection in the bug box, I lined a cardboard box with plastic and dumped into it a couple of buckets of compost and damp, rich earth, so that she could find tinier wrigglies for the babe. My fears proved to be groundless. Earthworms of any size, of course, were summarily rejected and the compost was soon incorporated into our games when County would bombard me with pieces of mouldy orange peel. But the preferred meals for the babe were flat brown centipedes nearly two inches long, which County pounded and folded into suitably sized morsels. And although I absolutely refused to let her feed the little one a small slug that first day (nothing seemed more indigestible to me), she fed her one the second day and gained her point—County knew more about feeding robin nestlings than I did. It's odd, really, that I would have to learn even that.

By the second day, the nestling's eye slits were gaining definition, and they continued to do so daily. Her skin along the edges of her tiny wings,and down the centre of her back darkened, rapidly as the feathers-to-be organized themselves inside in readiness for emerging. Just four days after hatching, only her head would have fit into her eggshell, and even moths and medium-sized worms joined the continual cavalcade of wrigglies down her throat. Being, like Bugs, the sole recipient of County's ardent mothering, the rotund babe seemed to my amused perceptions to bask in perpetual repletion, punctuated by polite responses to County's persistent offerings. Unable to resist, I named her Burp.

County, meanwhile, in addition to the feedings, broodings and fecal sac removals, daily aerated the bottom of the nest as she had done before. It occurred to me then, that perhaps the aerating not only allowed County's warmth to circulate, but also helped the babe to breathe while County warmed her. The nest itself, whenever I put my face into it, always smelled as sweet and fresh as new hay.

Old friends, however hopeful of seeing Burp at this stage, had no visiting privileges as far as County was concerned. Once, when one of them slipped cautiously into the room behind me, County, standing on the edge of the nest, eyed him coldly. When he tried stretching higher to see into the nest, she immediately stepped in and snuggled down over Burp in bristling indignation, averting her head pointedly, her eyes narrowed and her whole demeanour frosty. Reluctantly I beckoned the disappointed friend back out of the room. No matter how many bottles of flies he had generously provided over the winter, a mother robin's will is law in her own territory.

For the first few days I left the infertile eggs in the nest with Burp, to lend lateral support, and she usually draped herself over them, with one pink winglet spread out on each egg, her heavy head tipped down between. When I removed the eggs on the fourth day during County's absence, Burp's eyes were already opening just a crack; unlike Bugs, whose eyes opened within a day, her eyes took a few days to open fully. By the fifth day she was sprinkled with tiny feather beginnings, and a week to the day, the feather shafts on her wings were tufted as the sheaths began to crumble. By then she was enthusiastically greeting each arrival of County's with piping cheeps of welcome.

Of course, as a new father once more, I was busily recording Burp's progress for the 'family album' and was highly amused when she began dropping down at the camera's click in the old familiar way. She seemed naturally timid, and less adventuresome than Bugs; as she began to perceive me clearly, she would crouch in the nest or in my hand soundlessly snapping her tiny beak and raising her feathers defensively—for all the world like a diminutive feathered snapping turtle. As the days passed though, I began to worry about her lack of initiative. At ten days of age and beautifully feathered as well, she should have been preening frequently, exercising her wings, and showing every inclination to explore beyond the nest. Would she have been more stimulated if she'd had siblings to contend with instead of inert eggs?

I began to set her on my lap, patting and tickling her and gently prodding her up on her feet; in general, trying to imitate the jostling action of siblings. Her legs weren't strong and her balance was shaky, forcing her to shoot out one or both wings frequently for stability. But she responded wonderfully to this stimulation: trying short walks, preening, and even beating her wings with eyes bright with excitement while I steadied her body. From a day of lap sessions we advanced to a warm couch cushion under a lamp, where I'd leave her on her own between feedings and exercises. She progressed very rapidly, wing-beating, scratching, preening and even attempting to oil her feathers. Her curiosity, too, unfolded quickly—even alarmingly. I began to scrutinize the household arrangements again with an eye oriented towards possible disasters. The metal heat shield around the woodstove required thick padding along the sharp upper edge, and the coiled handles on the stove doors, so menacing to small legs and toes, were each embellished with a bright woolen mitten for the duration of the summer—a waving, whimsical touch. Tall boots were laid on their sides, and all nestling-swallowing crevices at either end of the couch were stuffed with spare bedding. It was the countdown to launching.

County, meanwhile, had begun speculative nestbuilding activities the day I took Burp out of the nest for exercises. When I began leaving her on the couch cushion, County progressed to demolishing and rebuilding the nest over the next two days, leaving more of Burp's feedings and training to me. Whenever I headed outside to gather insects, I'd set Burp into last year's cowskull nest, which still hung over the couch, and she'd nestle in comfortably till I returned. I worried about leaving her down on the couch since one of the red squirrels frequenting the feeding stations occasionally followed its curious nose through crevices in the screened porch to the living room, where I'd find it sitting up rather charmingly in the garden. Unfortunately, small birds are squirrel food—which isn't nearly so charming.

By this time I had concluded that Burp was a female. Her head had the same colouring as Towne's and County's at that age, whereas Bugs had had a noticeably darker head. This was later confirmed when Burp moulted to her adult plumage.

The new nest being damp with constant applications of fresh mud and wet grasses, Burp slept by herself in the old cowskull nest. Shortly after I had initiated her exercises, she suddenly became mobile—running and tumbling all over the couch and table, the floor and garden. Her strength seemed to have instantly doubled, and she began using her wings for short lifts to higher spots. Even the window ledges became accessible to her, and one of her favourite areas for resting.

I began placing her in the flat water dish several times, trying to teach her to drink, but the feel of wetness spooked her. She grew less nervous about it as I persisted, and would watch, fascinated, as I splashed the surface with one finger, but would veer aside when I gently pushed her head down to drink. I couldn't climb in to demonstrate, and County was in her nest building blur, so I began playing with Burp's toes under the water. My touch caused her to peer down curiously, thus dipping her beak into the water. Her surprise was quickly surpassed by pure delight,—and she drank deeply again and again like a little feathered dromedary that had finally staggered into a welcome oasis. She was endearingly awkward—stretching her head well out in front, her eyes wide open as she nibbled the air rapidly in search of water, while gradually lowering her beak. Sometimes she stopped and drew back without having wetted it, and other times would grab the water determinedly, with sneezes being her only reward. The difficulty with still water is that it's invisible. But her perseverence finally satisfied her thirst, and a new threshold of perplexity had been passed.

Burp was a beautiful fledgling with a pale, buff-coloured, speckled front and unusual, finely-chiselled features—different again from all the others. As she stood dipping her beak within the widening rings of sparkling water, sunlight slanting through the greenery and shimmering around her delicate form, she personified the universal spirit of youth and innocence, ever renewed by the boundless waters of the Source. Afterward, she perched in the garden, contentedly pouring out the uplifting notes and trills so characteristic of thrush songs—her first effort, a melodic fragment of the universal song.

CHAPTER 12

BACK TO THE WILD

THREE WEEKS TO THE DAY THAT BURP HATCHED, County laid the first egg of her second clutch, following two days of charming courtship at 5:30 a.m. on my pillow. Again, her happiness was so manifest that I could tell by the expression in her eyes that she was warming an egg. The next day's egg brought great restlessness and increased discomfort before it finally arrived, but her third and fourth eggs came normally and she settled down contentedly to steady brooding and wild games. I too maintained a steady round of hunting insects, cleaning, and supervising Burp, as well as frequent forays into the woods armed to the teeth against mosquitoes, while I searched for another fertile egg. A father's work is never done.

In the meantime, Burp's daily discoveries were a constant delight to witness. Her coordination improved quickly, which merely changed the nature of her predicaments but failed to eliminate them. Advancing from tumbles into the leafy embrace of a date palm in the garden, she gained enough wing power to ascend to the loft railing—only to be marooned up there, saucer-eyed and speechless, until I located her and carried her back downstairs. Responding nestily to the encircling warmth of my hands, she would often snuggle down in them for a cozy nap, and at dusk would protest strongly to roosting all alone. When her crop was full, she would be moved to song, and early one morning I was astonished to hear her produce the migratory 'whistle—bark, bark, bark' call which County had discarded since the beginning of the nesting season.

To my immense relief, one of her quicker achievements was in feeding herself. Of course she refused earthworms, and also slugs, but adored mealworms and cheese, which she began to pick up with minimal persuasion from me, standing well back from the dish and reaching forward tentatively with the tip of her beak. Once, when I lifted her up beside a window on a finger-perch, she caught a fly. After a couple of days, she began frequenting the bug box and making awkward grabs at the inhabitants, with occasional success. Her focus, as it had been with the Swainson's thrushes, appeared to be sowbugs, it being within her power to catch them. The brown centipedes, which she also loved, were too fast, so I would catch her one now and then—when they weren't too fast for me.

I watched her one day, perched on the rim of the bug box, the picture of intense concentration as she studied the variety of wrigglies below. She reminded me of a kingfisher watching a pool. Then she spotted a sowbug, and highly excited, leaned more and more forward, reaching down eagerly with her beak until she fell straight in on her head with a thump—but emerged victoriously clutching the sowbug.

Early each morning when I opened the porch 'trap' to County, I would ride Burp up and down the screens on my finger. She quickly gained proficiency in grabbing the moths fluttering before her eyes. In time she began catching the brown centipedes in the bug box, and I was floored one day when she defended the bug box against County who'd suddenly arrived while Burp was on the hunt. When County objected but left Burp in triumphant possession, I wondered if I'd ever be surprised at anything again. Subsequent reflection convinced me that County was reinforcing Burp's display of maturity and confidence, just as she would reinforce Burp's lack of speed and efficiency in eating by stealing an oversize bug Burp was contemplating on the floor before her. Burp soon became very quick at disposing of her prey.

One of Burp's most exhilarating discoveries, though, was the sun bath. She was initiating her own water baths now, but one bright morning I set her down on a hot sunny window sill. It was a happy idea. Burp instantly became mesmerized by the sensation of enveloping warmth. Her head feathers rose while her eyes grew round and fixed. Then her body feathers lifted as well, letting the heat seep luxuriously into her skin. With enthusiastic abandon, she spread out both wings and tail, gazed unblinkingly into the sun, and sprawled with her beak wide open, drinking in the heat. The sunlight pouring into her mouth glowed redly behind her transparent throat feathers in delicate, unearthly beauty as she remained there, completely intoxicated and motionless. During the next quarter of an hour she baked, changing sides as needed, her breathing rapid and shallow, and utter enjoyment radiating from every hot feather. I began to see humorous images of robins basking on Florida beaches between migrations, and placing orders for chilled drinks. Concerned finally that she might overindulge, I reluctantly broke the spell by carrying her off bodily, still glorying in sunglow, to the shadiness of the garden, where she refreshed herself with a cool drink and a preen. Burp had become an ardent sunworshipper.

FOUR days after County's clutch was complete, I once more replaced two of her infertile eggs with a fertile one. Again the egg was removed from the wild nest while the female was off feeding so as not to distress her unduly. And again, both the wild female and County continued to brood their altered clutches. Job sharing was definitely catching on.

Five days later, as though sensing something, I decided to visit County at her nest late in the afternoon, setting aside my work in the other part of the house. She was on her eggs but I could hear a steady peeping, which for a moment I attributed to Burp who was nearby. But just as I realized that both Burp and County were silent, County stood up and clucked—and I became transfixed. The peeping was coming from one of the eggs, which was encircled with an irregular crack. At that moment, one end of the shell broke away from the other and a tiny robin thrust his head up and immediately gaped. I was utterly astounded—not even a moment of recovery was necessary for this newest member of the family. I guessed that he was a male which, be it coincidence or otherwise, turned out to be correct.

Burp was highly intrigued with the new arrival. She spent a

good part of each day beside the nest watching all the activity, but showed no inclination to brood the babe herself, as Bugs had. County was again in her glory feeding and warming her latest, and keeping the nest clean and aerated. She swooped Burp rather frequently, even trouncing her a few times when they were both in the garden or near the bugbox, but accepted her presence by the nest quite peacefully. After a few days, I removed the infertile eggs during one of the feeding sessions, but was struck by County's sudden expression of anxiety. Then she seemed to accept the situation as she settled down in the nest to warm the babe, turning her head away as she did so. I wondered if I should have removed them when she was absent, as I had done before, but didn't feel comfortable about that method either, since it seemed underhanded. It was an issue I continued to ponder.

Meanwhile, the height of my personal ambitions had dwindled to the modest aspiration of gathering enough wrigglies on each outing for the larder so that I wouldn't need to forage more than five times a day—my life consisting of other demands as well. The porch trap was still yielding fairly well each morning, and the little one flourished on bristling mouthfuls of breakfast moths from County's sunrise scrounging. In addition, an enterprising young friend had presented me with an ingenious contrivance consisting of a black-light bulb to attract moths, and a fan to blow them down into a one-way holding net. I'd plug this in at dusk on the opposite side of the house from the porch trap and early each morning shake the moths out of the net and into the porch with the others. It augmented our bug supply wonderfully.

But now, County showed an insistent distaste for feeding the babe the sowbugs and slugs she had fed Burp—perhaps they were more flavourful in the spring than the summer. Desperation forced me to add them to my bucket anyway whenever I encountered them. Earthworms, of course, she discarded as well—I began to think of them as the poor man's hamburger. Given lean steak at the same price, they'd never eat hamburger again. Worms perhaps are never desirable; just an unavoidable necessity with the fluctuating availability of tastier tidbits. With such added restrictions, I began to experience considerable difficulty in maintaining the variety of wrigglies County demanded. She did show tremendous enthusiasm for green caterpillars which were nearly impossible for me to find, though I hunted diligently. Flat brown centipedes were still high on the list of favourites, but as the summer grew hotter and drier, my usual damp, crawly haunts yielded fewer and fewer. As even the compost became less disgusting to examine, it became less worth examining. Only the hordes of mosquitos and black flies swarmed around me, as merrily as ever. With all my sources drying up, and the appetites of all three robins not in the least diminished, the hours needed each day to provide food for them gradually lengthened. I would have taken out a second mortgage for a daily supply of cutworms—*delivered.*

As the days passed, Burp brooded the babe only once and rather briefly but her fascination persisted. Unfortunately, I was obliged to discourage her nestside visits. If she was nearby when County was off gathering food, the little one, dozing languidly in the nest and perhaps mistaking Burp's movements for County's, would immediately gape in the delicious expectation of being fed. Burp's outlandish response, for reasons never made clear to me, was to reach over and seize the baby's beak in a gentle but inexorable grip. This was disconcerting enough for him when his eyes were open. When they were unopened, it was terrifying, and his shrill squeak would bring County back in a flash. Burp never indicated any malicious intent, and certainly County never drove her from the nest, which seemed to reinforce my interpretation. But as it began to happen more frequently, I worried that the nestling's beak might suffer irreparable damage, however unintentionally acquired, and began to distract Burp with other interests whenever I saw her near the nest. Anyway, with County chasing her more often, and the little one already ten days old and almost ready to emerge from the nest, I realized that the time had come for Burp to leave us. She was feeding herself perfectly and was very adept in flight; soon the babe would be under his father's 'wing,' while his mother began a new nest and laid another clutch of eggs. It was time for Burp to be on her own.

EARLY one morning, after I'd gathered enough food to keep County and her babe content for a few hours, I took Burp outside for the first time. It was difficult to believe that she was already five weeks old—time seemed to drag interminably only when I was gathering bugs. I squatted down and began prodding the earth and turning over leaves with my 'finger beak' in the same way that I'd first taught Burp when she was new to the world beyond the nest. She joined in immediately, swallowing whatever she found, even earthworms, with a singularly serious air, as though we'd left playtime on the other side of the door. Her sudden earnestness seemed so at variance with her innate juvenile charm, as though she were abruptly donning the responsibilities of adulthood, in defiance of her brief existence and experience—as indeed she was. I realized then she hadn't just grown bigger—she'd grown up.

We spent nearly the whole day together learning—sometimes on the ground, sometimes on the roof, a glorious elevation where I sang old childhood songs to Burp—songs that her dad sang when he was a little girl. I also witnessed her ecstasy as she flew freely out around an enormous matriarchal spruce and back again. Landing beside me each time with an accomplished thump, she'd look at me with eyes radiating excitement and happiness, while I lauded her efforts and shared her delight. I left her outside on her own several times, but checked constantly from the windows. She seemed to be enjoying the adventure immensely, without any indication of fear. Her reactions, even when chased out of another robin's territory, were quick and skilfull; unquestionably confident. Her mottled camouflage was wonderful against the old, gray, weathered spruces—twiggily protective and encrusted with lichens and trailing beards, and even yet I pick her out only with difficulty in colour photos. Hunger sent her periodically back down to the ground to hunt for bugs where again, her russet, gray and white patterns disguised her where-abouts effectively enough to send me searching anxiously from window to window. No doubt the keener, hungry eyesight of a sharp-shinned hawk would spot her more quickly but, hopefully, her own keen vision would come to her aid—as well as her innate lightning reflexes. I had known countless occasions when County has seen something, reacted, and then counter-reacted—all in an instantanous processing of information, the finalization of which gave me the sluggish impression that something of note had occurred. There's nothing like watching a robin's reactions to make me feel about as perceptive as a mothball.

Towards evening, Burp sat for a long time, rather dangerously exposed, on the very peak of the roof in a mild steady drizzle. I wondered where she'd choose to spend the night. No other inde-pendent juveniles with practical roosting experience that Burp could share had appeared and, as the light began to fail, I heard her calling. I went out immediately, standing within her view to speak reassuringly to her. After a few moments, she flew down onto my shoulder and I decided to take her in for the night. But as I entered the living room with Burp still on my shoulder, County instantly attacked her, with the same vehemence with which she used to attack Bang. Just as Burp's leaving the nest, even for part of the day, had terminated her nestlinghood in County's eyes, leaving County free to prepare for the next family, so Burp's departure from the home territory was considered final. Her unscheduled return was an infringement of territorial rights, as by any other intruder, and was treated accordingly. County's belligerence did not find expression in the mild trouncings of even the previous day, when Burp was still her offspring, but was executed with serious intent, as toward a stranger. Being only an honorary robin and not feeling qualified to contest the point, I segregated Burp in the porch until dark, then sneaked her in to her usual roost once County was settled for the night on her nest, a quietly-closed door separating her from Burp. Next morning, as soon as it was light, I slipped Burp back out to the porch before opening County's door. Spouses can't always be in each other's confidence.

After enjoying a short visit and a breakfast of mealworms, Burp began to get restless; so I opened the outside door again and out she flew. I left the door ajar for some time afterward, keeping the inner door to the living room closed, and in less than an hour Burp returned briefly before leaving forever. I caught an occasional glimpse of her throughout the day, but had no idea where she spent the night. She must have chosen her roost wisely though, because early the following morning, as I stepped out in full bug-hunting regalia, there was Burp high up in the corner tree with several jays, all warming themselves in the early glory of the sun. And although she watched me as I saluted her joyfully, she made no attempt to join me. Nor did I give her any encouragement to do so.

Later that day when I was busy inside, a robin spoke outside and both County and I instantly answered. Although we'd heard robin calls all day our reaction to this particular voice was so spontaneous that there was no question in my mind that we were answering Burp. I would be totally unable to describe just how her voice was to be distinguished from the others; but then, neither could I describe the voice of a particular human friend so that even a mutual aquaintance could indentify it.

Throughout the rest of that summer, I caught periodic sightings of Burp, noting her gradual change to female adult plumage, with the head feathers, as usual, being the last to moult—and somehow invariably conveying the impression of her head being a size too small. I looked for her with great anxiety after thunderstorms or high winds, and was greatly relieved when I was finally rewarded with the delight of seeing her eating chokecherries with complete unconcern or sunbathing with the jays up in the corner tree. Later in the fall, I saw her enjoying the indigo berries on the Virginia creeper, her plumage (except for her head)

Weed stretching his new wing feathers (above) and peeking out between County's legs as she aerates the nest (right). (Flash photos were taken with the flash deflected off white cardboard to protect the nestlings' eyes.)

Weed out of the nest (left).

*Burp's marvellous return in the fol-
lowing spring outside the dining
room window (below).*

County's little family thrived beautifully (above).

A close-up of County feeding (right).
Notice how far her beak is pushed
into the nestling's throat. Since she
would do this to one or two babes
before unloading food into the third,
this may have been her way of deter-
mining who was to be fed by the
fullness of each crop.

The timeless miracle of hatching (above). Photos of nest interiors were shot into a handheld mirror above the nest with 1000 speed film.

Twelve days later, the babes were out of the nest and into the indoor garden (left).

County "preparing" wrigglies in the
earth-filled wading pool (above).

Co-ordination for the youngsters
was always full of surprises (right).

The mottled plumage of this released youngster blends well with the foliage (above).

Little Eyebrows came to me for food outside for about two weeks. This photo really shows how he came by his name (left).

County's unflagging nesting enthu-
siasm was evident to all (above).

The wonderful starry patterning on
Blimp's back (right).

Blimp had a curved bill like Towne and Bugs, but full eye-rings like County.
Her overall rotundity resulted in her unusual name.

beautiful, and her whole demeanour contented and confident—all of which was conclusive reinforcement of the efficacy of her unorthodox upbringing. She still showed no inclination to make contact with me, or to enter the porch, and I still refrained from making any overtures to her—her existence depended upon independence and self-reliance.

To me, the circle was complete. The awesome responsibility of removing a live egg from a wild robin's nest was now fulfilled with Burp's successful re-integration into the wild. It was possible for County to forego her natural heritage in order to stay with a human, and yet fully realize her maternal longings. And, most importantly, it was possible for her to do so not wholly at the expense of another female robin's own maternal aspirations, or of a young robin's chances for survival in the natural world.

CHAPTER THIRTEEN

THRESHOLDS

THE DAY FOLLOWING BURP'S DEPARTURE, I took the second nestling out of the nest, since County was showing great impatience to rebuild—even doing a little footwork while the babe was still in the nest. As soon as the way was clear, she not only began carrying up mud to that nest, but also up to the old cowskull nest as well, as though meditating a change of locale. I left her to it and concentrated my attention on the little one's needs—even arranging a little canopied nest on the back of the couch out of an arrangement of cushions in which he spent the next few nights, both nests being damp with mud.

He was a most endearing creature, and different again in appearance and personality from those who had preceded him. His breast was a deep, rich orange, liberally flecked with dark spots, but even the touches of contrast around his eyes and in his wing feathers were orange, rather than white—an interesting variation. Being a male, his head feathers were much darker than Burp's—the same dark colouring as Bugs had had. His habitual expression, though, was singular. I can only describe it as a most charming perpetual smile. His nature matched his smile in its innate, easy-going placidity. He encountered each day's perplexities with the same enviably pleasant demeanour, and never appeared anxious or distressed. The learning process for him was a delightful glide through interesting scenes, and he remained wholly untouched by the sometimes feverish activities encircling him. His contentedness found expression in ongoing minute high-pitched squeaks and warbles whenever he was cradled in my hands. I fell quite naturally into the habit of calling him Squeek.

County, meanwhile, left Squeek's upkeep to me and threw herself frenziedly into nest building, centering finally on the cowskull location. I remember being quite struck by her excessive, almost desperate drive, with energy more applicable to the first clutch of the season, not the third. Her feverish zeal was even noticed by friends, but none of us considered any other possible explanation than the normal eagerness for motherhood.

But the difficulty in gathering enough insects was becoming acute for me. Summer was at the full, and the dampest areas I could find were scarce in insects—but plentiful in replete salamanders. Even the porch trap and the black light trap were yielding only a few moths each morning. I began driving once more to yards of friends, meticulously overturning deep accumulations of wood chips in firewood storage areas, the favourite haunt of centipedes, as well as picking through composts. I still found little, and the little I did find, in the composts particularly, consisted of earthworms. Being under the necessity of feeding Squeek and teaching him to feed himself, I resorted to taking him with me which, luckily, was fine by County—Squeek enjoyed himself wherever he was. The only difficulty was that my prolonged absence caused County alarm, this period being one of frequent close courtship. She would greet me with anxious courting gestures on my return. Four days after Burp's return to the wild, County laid the first egg of her third clutch but she engaged in only sporadic brooding. The next day's egg found her brooding more steadily, while the third egg, after unusual discomfort, perhaps due to its sandpapery texture, completed her setting.

During the days of County's laying, Squeek gradually became very subdued and difficult to feed, turning his head to avoid food and spitting it out whenever I successfully filled his throat. He seemed as benign as ever, and his efforts at beginning to fly were successful. But he clearly craved attention between frequent periods of dozing—a significant communication which I only understood later. The summer weather was hot and intensely humid, to which I attributed his sluggishness, and I tried to coax him into bathing, or at least cooling his feet in the waterdish. His appetite revived one evening when the temperature dropped, and remained good. But oddly enough, this same day, after she laid her last egg, County resumed feeding Squeek herself, continuing to do so through the following two days which I linked with her impatience for motherhood, not sensing any other connection. I was relieved to be free of the responsibility, as I was intensely occupied with gathering bugs wherever I could, but by the end of the third day of her feedings, I knew Squeek was ill. He sat motionless, his eyes tightly closed in an unending doze, his cheeriness dissolved, and his droppings yellow and strong-smelling. I began treating him with tetracycline; by evening, his droppings were normal and he was gaping for food. But by the following morning he was terribly weak and ill, and lay suffering in my hands. Then for a few moments, he suddenly became painfree. His eyes opened to me and his lost smile returned, completely transforming his expression. Shortly after, he passed away. County had been watching from her nest and had flown over to him as he lay in my hands, but now she sat quietly on her eggs, still watching, her eyes dark and serious.

Squeek's death was a mystery to me. Could I inadvertently have fed him unsuitable food—an insect that birds in the wild would never eat? County's judgment in such matters I trusted implicitly. But I didn't possess the judgment of a robin. Could there have been an internal physical flaw which would have terminated his life at this point even in the wild? Although I made enquiries, I was politely discouraged from having an autopsy performed due to the difficulties in transporting Squeek in as fresh a state as possible to the nearest facility in the province.

With great sadness, I buried him beneath the spruce trees—evergreen in remembrance.

DURING the next week and a half, County brooded her eggs while I brooded Squeek's passing. In between, we still played wild games, and were rewarded with brief glimpses of Burp who was obviously doing well—a reassuring note.

Then, about this time, a friend driving home from work spotted a small fledgling sitting by the roadside. Not willing to leave him in such a dangerous place and unable to see any adult birds nearby, my friend dropped him off to me. The little creature sat in my hand with complete composure, emitting at frequent intervals what I could only term a short but piercing howl. County was outraged and refused to tolerate his presence at all, making her displeasure perfectly clear by swooping us both and shrieking angrily. I sat the placid little stranger on a windowsill in a separate room, closed the door, and hunted through the bird books, trying to identify the source of those periodic howls still ringing out so persistently. I made no headway whatsoever, and thus was puzzled what to feed him, although his substantial beak seemed to suggest seeds. But County's indignation promised unending difficulties in keeping him, even temporarily. Then I got an idea.

I telephoned the friend who'd brought him and got a clear description of the precise location on the dirt road where he'd found the babe. I drove there, and for the next quarter of an hour, strolled up and down the area, cradling the fledgling. He gave no indication of uneasiness, but continued to howl loudly with strikingly calm assurance. Suddenly I heard a faint answer, and the babe instantly reacted with even louder quickened reponses. I was delighted—and nearly deafened. It made me grateful for my own quieter thrush 'offspring.'

Finally I saw one of the parents—a beautiful male rose-breasted grosbeak. The mystery guest was identified at last. Quickly I set the babe high on a branch well back from the road, and retreated to the truck, where I watched their eager reunion before driving contentedly home. After directing a searching look of suspicion at me, but finding me unaccompanied, County too was content.

ALTHOUGH I was having no luck at all in my paternal responsibilities of locating another wild nesting robin, I did have a breakthrough in my bug-gathering problems—a butterfly net. With this I wandered several times a day through the wild tangled meadows, sweeping the net back and forth through the grasses and bushes, and dumping my catch on the table inside the screened porch—that was screened originally to keep bugs *out*—where they swarmed everywhere. Eventually I replaced the netting with a pillow case pinned to the hoop, which eliminated snagging and tearing on thorns and spiky stalks and prevented escapees. County was delighted with this innovation, which blessed her with such delicious hordes of grasshoppers, spiders, caterpillars, leafhoppers, occasional butterflies, and a whole range of wrigglies that I had rarely made accessible to her before. Monarch butterflies I avoided because of their toxic nature. As soon as I passed through the house with the loaded net, she would sweep off her nest and follow me to the porch, where she darted excitedly amongst her scrambling prey, snapping up special favourites in every direction. The net method, besides being more efficient was a lot easier on me, involving merely a few pleasant walks in meadows each day rather than long hours of crouching and aching for disappointingly small quantities of earthier insects. I began to dimly recall those far-off days, as though in a previous lifetime, when I used to carry insects *out* of the house, releasing them gently where they could survive. Not that my actions now were really questionable—accepting the responsibility of a robin's care included the responsiblity of providing proper food—fortunately, it needn't include witnessing the food being pounded or crunched into suitable mouthfuls.

Two weeks after County's last egg was laid, I finally found a wild robin's egg for her and managed the exchange in the same unobtrusive manner as before, both robins continuing to brood their respective clutches. But the same evening I made the switch, I noticed County examining her eggs very closely, and cocking her head close to them as though listening. When she snuggled back down over them, it was with fresh pleasure, as though she'd finally sensed the changes of life and growth. I was relieved, since she had brooded so long that I wondered if she might give up just as I'd finally gotten her an egg.

Three days later in the morning, County, to my surprise, was tapping quite firmly on one of the eggs—which I'd never known her to do before. The hatching proved to be an unusually long and difficult procedure this time, the eggshell perhaps being thicker than usual. Possibly, too, County could hear prolonged ineffectual struggling which required outside assistance, and through verbal communications with the inmate, his inability to make headway was made clear. In any case, she and the babe both cooperated, and finally the eggshell separated to reveal a tiny, damp, exhausted nestling who was too feeble yet to lift his head and gape, as Squeek had done. Eventually, he managed to push the upper portion of shell further away with his head, and County removed it. But although he rested frequently and was warmed each time by County, extricating himself from the bottom shell was such a long arduous process that when I judged it was safe to interfere, I removed it myself. He was still too weak to lift his head, and at County's cluck would struggle a little, but finally remain sprawling, gaping hopefully where he lay. So very gently indeed, and trying to avoid pressure on those fragile, bulbous, closed eyes, I held his head up with fingers that suddenly resembled tree trunks. County, holding food, clucked, the miniature beak opened, and the babe was fed. Each feeding thereafter was accomplished with the same teamwork. By late afternoon he was able to manage two feedings without my assistance, and his constant cheep underneath County got stronger and steadier. The next day he required no assistance whatever from me, and grew daily at such an outlandish rate that I called him 'Weed.' I couldn't help reflecting what Weed's early chances for survival would have been under natural conditions, and whether he could have held his own with more vigorous siblings. Could any other father robin have held his head up?

The days immediately following Weed's hatching were so distressingly hot (32°C) that even walking the meadows with the bug net was utterly exhausting—and futile. I discovered that the wiser field wrigglies preferred to emerge during the relatively cooler mornings and evenings, and thankfully, I joined them. I also discovered that County dribbled saliva periodically into Weed's mouth—presumably to prevent his dehydration, as these were the hottest days we'd encountered yet this year. I had never seen her do this before, but then, she hadn't had a featherless nestling during such intense heat before, either. The ingenuity and simplicity of the method impressed me, and I fancied myriads of other helpless youngsters being relieved simultaneously with liquid refreshment while heat waves shimmered over the fields and the very forest gasped for cooler air.

Weed thrived heartily despite the hot weather, and his eyes were open by the time he was a week old. His feathers grew with indecent haste. County often prevented overwarming him by simply standing above him and sitting on him only when more heat was required. My fatherly interest in family photos caught several of Weed peeking back out between County's legs. On one occasion when County was settled over him, Weed's head was protruding from under her front feathers as he dozed, his beak resting comfortably on the rim of the nest. Just as I focused in on his face, he gave a most prodigious yawn and slithered down out of sight under County's feathers.

He began preening when only a week old, and at ten days his tailfeathers were already half an inch long. He was also stretching, standing and wingbeating constantly, had a ferocious appetite, and was highly intrigued with activities beyond the nest. His breast was a rich orange similar to Squeek's, but his eyerings and the touches of contrast in his wings were white like Burp's. His head feathers were very dark, proclaiming him a male in the same way as Squeek and Bugs. Weed's restlessness in the confines of the nest increased daily, although he hesitated to emerge on his own. So finally, at thirteen days I set him out on the couch. County had again been instigating nestbuilding while he was still underfoot, and I was trying firmly to discourage her from another clutch. All fathers have their limits.

The first day that Weed was out of the nest was a happy one for him. He was immediately mobile, hopping all over the garden and the rest of the living room in great spirits. Even hopping through the waterdish proved to be exciting, and worthy of several repetitions; by late afternoon I wasn't surprised to find him sleepy and subdued. But when he began to spit out his feedings I became highly uneasy, my thoughts reverting to Squeek's similar symptoms. And with good reason.

The next morning, he was changed. He refused food and was very subdued. With an anxious heart, I set him on top of a favourite driftwood perch, and was dismayed when he produced a small, yellowish, strong-smelling dropping. Very shortly thereafter, he fell off. A few minutes later, as I held him close, fighting the inevitable, he died.

This time, angrily overriding all obstacles, I engaged someone to drive him the necessary distance for an autopsy. I packed him in a thermally-controlled styrofoam container equipped with an ice pack and also included the yellow dropping in a sterile jar. I added droppings from County and the pigeons for analysis. I absolutely refused to leave County, because I had ascertained that she had cleaned the nest of his droppings by swallowing them, causing her own droppings to assume that fatal yellow hue and strong odour.

The cause of death given for both Weed (and therefore Squeek) was coccidiosis, a host-specific disease contracted by fecal-oral transmission. County was also infected, but her adult strength gave her the required resistance. As recommended, I dosed her successfully with Amprollium. Desmond and Molly tested clear. (Incidentally, the findings also confirmed that Weed was indeed a male.) The answer to the cause of Weed's death, far from lightening the cloud of mystery, darkened it. Coccidiae bacteria, I was told, are found normally in most living creatures, but only increase to dangerous proportions under stress. I had always associated the disease with poultry, and remembered taking Squeek with me to a grassy farmyard with free-ranging hens in order to gather bugs. Could he have been infected there? No, I was told, not unless I had fed him with food visibly smeared with yellowish, foul-smelling droppings. Not only had I not done so, I hadn't seen any such droppings there. I was also told that if that farm flock had been infected, their young would not survive. There had been many youngsters there in perfect health, not to mention wild birds in the usual numbers.

I reconsidered stress. If it were stress, and originated with County, changing her coccidiae count to levels that young birds couldn't combat, how could her droppings contaminate the nestlings? Could the disease possibly have originated in Squeek, contaminating County as she removed or swallowed his droppings, causing her in turn to infect Weed? If so, what stressed Squeek, and at such a young age? The baby thrushes would have been likelier candidates for stress reaction, after their experience prior to their adoption by County. And if the disease did begin with County, what stress was she under? Nothing made her happier than motherhood. One of the vets I consulted questioned me most particularly as to possible acute anxiety she might have been experiencing. I could think of nothing at the time. But gradually, through the ensuing months, an idea germinated.

Nothing made her happier than motherhood. Her eager anticipation with each setting of eggs could not be denied; I had closely shared those moments every time. But what of her emotions with all the eggs that didn't hatch? She had laid fourteen eggs and had raised three babies. I recalled the anxiety she had so clearly expressed when I had removed the infertile eggs before her eyes. I also recalled her intense joy with each hatching and her almost feverish drive this summer, increasing rather than abating—yet each clutch yielded only one babe in spite of all her efforts. I felt I had a clue to the mystery.

I have never ascribed to the oft-established maxim that birds can't count—only to the obvious conclusion that they can't convince *us* that they can; not even to touch upon other possible approaches to counting we might not perceive, such as inner 'photographic' images of the number of eggs in a clutch. I can glance at a printed paragraph for only a moment without moving my eyes—yet have read it. A fellow human might conclude, by observation alone, that I was illiterate. Birds that can achieve the monumental feat of migration over thousands of miles, seeing the route for the very first time, and yet reappearing at the 'family tree' where they were hatched, should not be so easily underestimated. In concentrating on County's capacity for happiness, I had underestimated her equal capacity for grief.

I determined to provide County the following summer with babies to match the eggs, as would be natural. I had previously chosen to supply single nestlings not only to appease my conscience towards the wild robins but because of the difficulties I knew I'd experience gathering enough bugs for whole families. County was my trust, and I knew perfectly well that nothing made her happier than motherhood. I realized painfully that I had shortchanged her.

Therefore I planned, with gritted teeth, that she would enjoy full families the following summer, if I had to spend my entire waking moments gathering bugs to ensure it. After all, I had friends with bug-ridden yards I could raid. The problem of how I was to give her the delight of a full family without depriving any wild robins of their equal rights I hoped to solve by springtime. I also determined to have her droppings analyzed prior to the nesting season, as well as periodically throughout the summer, and those of the nestlings done as well. A little advance planning in the bug-catching realm would definitely help too—perhaps another variety to cultivate like the mealworm culture.

Pre-natal classes were never like this.

CHAPTER FOURTEEN

NEW EXPERIENCES

THIS CONCLUSION, HOWEVER, TOOK THE WINTER MONTHS to crystallize. During the days following Weed's passing, County persisted in trying to build another nest for a fourth clutch of eggs, and I persisted in my efforts to deter her. Fear of contagion made me insist that no more hatchings be considered until the coccidiosis mystery was resolved. I concentrated on intensive cleaning throughout the house. It might be supposed with free-flying birds that the house resembled a neglected poultry shed, but this was not the case. I have an innate abhorrence of dirt and disorder, and although at peak busy times accumulated droppings would get ahead of me, the situation never remained that way for long. All flat surfaces had been recovered with materials that quickly wiped clean, the floors were mopped frequently, the furniture had washable coverings and even the earth in the garden was entirely replaced once a year. That friends didn't hesitate to dine with me seemed a clear indication that the premises must be socially and hygienically acceptable—some of the diners were even biologists.

County's unsatisfied motherhood, however, strove to find fulfillment. I hid the cowskull nest in the same room as the previous nests, bolting the door in spite of her protests. In retaliation, she began building on top of the handhewn beam in the livingroom. I couldn't lock that out of sight, so I tried discouraging her with squirts from the plant mister. But she persisted. I even let the dirt dry out in the garden and removed all nesting material that I could see, but she always managed to find threads or bits of paper somewhere. I cut back on wild food considerably, leaving her a diet mainly of mealworms and moths, in case added stimulation was coming from that quarter—but all in vain. Oddly enough, she never indicated any resentment towards my stubbornness— our spouseship was inviolable. I finally desisted, for fear of causing more coccidiosis complications through stressful frustration, and concluded that it might be more beneficial to her to let the cycle run its course. Four days after Weed's passing, County was again brooding three eggs, but anticipation of the disappointment in store for her gave me much unrest.

Nearly three weeks later, at two in the morning, County finally abandoned her clutch of eggs with evident distress and low barks of disturbance. I sat long with her trying to offer comfort, and finally coaxed her into accepting a few mealworms. But her distress persisted through the days that followed, with frequent displays of dissatisfaction and fussiness. Occasionally she lingered by the nest, or tore up a little nesting material; her general mood was most unhappy. The whole sense of unfulfillment left its mark throughout the rest of the year. Gone were a lot of the winter games we'd always played, and although she eventually stabilized, and always enjoyed feasts of mealworms, sharing my meals, prodding fresh loads of dirt in the garden, or just napping with me, her overall personality was subdued. Even her natural cycles were disturbed—she began her migration directly after the last clutch, perhaps a timely outlet for her thwarted energies, and failed to moult until October—a far cry from her usual August moult. Not until the light began to lengthen as spring approached, did she regain the high spirits of previous years.

The winter's events reinforced my conclusion that County required full families during her nesting times, so that none of this energy would remain at the end, to be vented in frustration and unhappiness. I resolved to make a much larger bug box, so that she would spend more energy hunting food for the babes, as would be natural, and also that I would remove the old nest after each session, so that the new nest would be built entirely from the beginning. Perhaps these measures, in addition to the labour of full families, would leave County exhausted but happy—as she had been the first year.

The more I learned from her, the more I realized how far I was from really understanding her deepest needs. But, as always, I determined to make her happiness a priority in spite of my blunderings. The persistence of her commitment to me—a unqualified privilege—made it mandatory.

BACK in the fall, I had loosed several dozen Old World crickets of all sizes and ages in the garden to add variety to County's diet, as well as to fulfill her natural desires to hunt insects, houseflies not being quite as plentiful this year. Although she ate a few of the adults, she soon preferred the littlest ones—less gristly, perhaps. The crickets eventually sought refuge from County's keen eye by hiding amongst the bricks under the woodstove, and I was pleasantly regaled with summer cricket music day and night all through the winter. The more daring of them climbed the walls, tumbled into mixing bowls in cupboards, wandered out to the pigeons' area, or sat singing overhead along the beam. Having crickets occasionally dropping down on me soon became the norm, and I found myself stepping carefully to avoid casualties. Visitors luxuriated in the surprise of being greeted with cricket music after braving sub-zero weather and stumbling through kneehigh snowdrifts. When I bottled a couple of brews of home-made beer, the crickets would line up on either side of escaping rivulets like cattle at a trough. Suppers were accompanied by insurpassable dinner music, and even my periodic bouts of insomnia became enjoyable. Whenever I felt stressed, I would sit beside the stove listening to the singing and watching in fascination as the crickets clambered energetically over the food mound, sometimes detouring around a very young mouse who often sat nearby, sharing their repast. They'd each choose particular tidbits to eat on the spot, or to lug back to their own special crevices in the bricks. Once, as I sat regarding three large adults clustered together sharing an especially-desirable tidbit, I was amused to watch a small youngster scurrying around and around them trying to join the feast, even passing under their bellies, before finally wedging in for his share.

I set out recumbent water bottles with cotton batting stoppers that allowed the crickets to suck out the water gradually (when

the mice didn't steal the cotton for their nests), and left a constant supply of pablum, dehydrated vegetable flakes, corn meal,
tropical fish food, sliced potatoes, crumbs from the bread board
and bits of my own suppers. The babies were particularly amazing—perfect, functioning crickets, less than a quarter of an inch
long. And another rarity—a pure white female with black eyes. I
started a second colony amongst some rocks in the garden, in the
hopes that they would lay eggs in the soil. Altogether, they were a
delightful addition to the family.

They were sometimes a humorous addition. Buying dry baby
food for them the first time left a memorable impression. An
enthusiastic young mother, seeing me pondering the bewildering
variety of products assembled before me, asked helpfully if 'it'
was a newborn. Cocking an amused eye at her, I replied drily,
"Some of them are."

As THE SOLSTICE turned and the light began to linger a little
longer each day, County's spirits began to rise. Early February
found her with gleaming eyes, giving mealworms deliberate
shakes and making a soft cluck deep in her throat—babies were
definitely on her mind. Throughout March she was swooping
excitedly through the house at sunrise, the rooms resounding
with her spring calls. I ruminated on the waiting hordes of shrill
mosquitoes that would also herald spring, and burrowed deeper
into the blankets, content to be comfortable as long as possible.
But with eager anticipation County began checking out possible
nesting sites, crouching experimentally in various locations, turning this way and that, and occasionally scratching about with her
feet. She began coaxing me constantly for extra attention, and
snuggled down in close companionship more and more frequently on my head. Her usual yearly cycles, though, were still disturbed, for she only began to 'migrate' ten days after the first
flocks of robins, grackles and blackbirds began to reappear among
the shrinking snow patches. And although her energies were
markedly lower than previous years, her redoubled appetite for

bugs was right on cue—even the less desirable adult crickets had to be nimble to escape. She quickly noted that whenever I misted the warm dry bricks beneath the woodstove, the crickets would emerge gratefully to lap up the moisture. After that, even if she was at the other end of the house, she'd come swooping as soon as she heard the plant mister and scuttle under the stove after her prey. The long, winter-warm days of basking tranquillity were definitely over for the crickets.

Mid-April arrived with mild sunny weather wilting the reluctant snow in even the deepest hollows, and allowing the woodland creatures to roam more freely. Unfortunately, some of them roamed a little too freely. I had just returned from a long, glorious walk rejoicing in the ever-magical renewal of spring, and was standing gazing out at the latest migrants feeding hungrily, when my rhapsodic musings were abruptly shattered. In turning from the window, I caught a brief glimpse of something passing the doorway into the dining-room.

"That wasn't a mouse," I thought, and at the same instant it passed back again. It was a snow-white weasel.

I was thunderstruck—and horrified. Weasels not only eat mice, but also birds. And, to state it mildly, weasels do not appreciate human interference at close range. Maneuvering after that weasel with knees of jelly wasn't easy, and for lack of a more sensible solution I grabbed the pillowcase net which I'd used last summer for catching insects. Catching a weasel in it was definitely going to be a challenge.

The weasel wasn't in the least perturbed by my sudden appearance with the net, but continued to slip silently and fluidly through the house, in and out of cupboards, and up on shelves, giving an occasional grunt and a dextrous twist whenever I shakily tried to net him. County swooped up to the loft, where she sat regarding this outlandish pantomine with considerable astonishment, tempered with alarm. At last, as I was at my wit's end, the weasel slipped into the bathroom, and I hastily wedged the door shut. Retrieving a large live-trap from the woodshed and baiting it with peanut butter—my reasoning being, that mice can be attracted by peanut butter and weasels are attracted by mice—I cautiously opened the door, shooed the weasel back in as he tried to escape, thrust in the trap and slammed the door. Music to my ears was the clang as the trap was sprung. Peering in carefully, I was delighted to see the culprit caged. Gingerly, I picked up the trap, and bolted to the truck, intending to drive a couple of miles before freeing him. I set the cage down on the passenger seat, turned the truck around and was heading down the road, when the weasel—with justifiable irritation—found a crevice in the trap and suddenly appeared directly beside me. Without the slightest presence of mind I instantly decamped, leaving the vehicle careening down the road with the door open, and a highly agitated weasel bobbing from window to window. In sudden dismay, I raced after the truck, succeeded in reaching in and jerking the shift into 'Park,' and then pulled open all the other doors. The weasel immediately fled to the woods, stopping only once to direct a brief look of horror in my direction before turning and vanishing. Hastily reparking, I ran back to the house to check on the birds. Going from room to room to count beaks, I was suddenly confronted once again with a snow-white weasel in the end room. I immediately slid the door shut which, it being a Japanese paper screen door, was more than ridiculous.

Now I was really in a quandary—unable to trap the weasel and unable to leave to get help. I began desperately phoning friends, most of whom appeared to have chosen that moment to be out. Eventually I tracked a couple down who came to my aid with weasel-proof live-traps and stalwart assistance in searching the room until we had located the mouse hole through which the second weasel had by then escaped. We surmised that they were a pair, and were strongly attracted to the smell of the mice which gained regular access to the house. Needless to say, I immediately launched an intensive campaign to stop up all mouse holes, and also to catch and release the resident mice to take up new quarters well down the road. I did so reluctantly because I'd often enjoyed the mice—watching County play chase with them in the garden, and being entranced by mouse mothers carrying little pink babies carefully in their mouths across the living room. But if the mice were going to attract weasels, the mice had to go.

The screen porch, too, had to be completely reinforced with strong wire mesh, plywood flooring and doors secure enough for the National Mint before I felt confident enough for the birds to use it. Seeing weasels in one's living room can definitely change one's life.

A MONTH after the weasel episode, and after a little speculative building in several locations simultaneously, County finally chose the cowskull again and threw herself daily into her nestbuilding fever, the gentler courtship rituals being reserved for sunrise on my pillow. I watched in considerable amusement as, with typical County enthusiasm, she killed a cricket and carried it up to her nest, clucking hopefully—and this when she'd laid only two of the three eggs comprising her first clutch. When the clutch was complete, she settled down contentedly to steady brooding punctuated with wild games of chase. This year our 'snatch and grab' game under the driftwood stump took on a new twist. Whenever I 'caught' County, I'd scoop her up gently in curved hands and toss her high into the air, to her unbounded delight. Often she'd scurry back under to be scooped up and tossed again and again—although I avoided such extremes whenever she was in an egg-laying cycle. I'd noticed how she cushioned her landings, as though feeling tender, when an egg was developing, and I was hesitant to handle her at those times.

I also took the precaution of having County's droppings analyzed for coccidiae and was dismayed to see a slight positive reading. I immediately treated her with Amprollium for three days, and in another three days tested her again. Thankfully, the reading this time was negative. After the sadness of the previous summer I was taking every precaution.

Just as County had completed her first clutch, we were both

delighted to welcome back Burp on the dining room windowsill. And Burp was obviously just as delighted to be there, running back and forth and trying repeatedly to fly inside. She was more reserved with me than with County, of course, and I didn't try to approach her outside, but contented myself with talking to her from inside. She quickly became more and more at ease with me. Her mate was with her and often Burp would be torn between gathering nesting material for her own mothering activities and flying up to the windowsill to visit. The two seemed to have claimed the immediate area around the house as their territory, and drove off bluejays that ventured too close. Burp then began a nest directly outside the dining room window in a huge matriarchal spruce but abandoned it—perhaps because of the proximity of squirrels and raccoons who haunted the feeding areas. She then completed a beautiful nest by the woodshed on the opposite side of the house but it was also abandoned, perhaps for the same reason. Eventually I lost sight of Burp and her mate and was unable to detect their final site. I did not see them again during the summer, although I often wondered if County knew of their activities. She would surely have recognized Burp's voice. Raising nestlings, I knew, is very intensive, and I hoped that all was well with them. That Burp had managed not only to migrate south for the first time as a juvenile, but to migrate north, all the way back to her 'family tree,' flying stoically through multiple hazards of traffic, pollution and predators, was such a stupendous accomplishment that I was completely in awe of the capabilities of this marvellous little creature—and had no doubts about her parenting abilities.

CHAPTER FIFTEEN

SPRING AGAIN

MEANWHILE, I WAS HUNTING DILIGENTLY FOR AN ACTIVE robin's nest in order to fulfill County's expectations of motherhood—without searching too near the house. I felt I really couldn't take Burp's eggs. I found nest after nest cunningly hidden in a variety of ways, but none were in use. The weather had become deplorably cold and wet, and constant clambering through dripping spruces quickly reduced me to sodden clothes, squelching boots, and chattering teeth. One bone-chilling afternoon found me plodding through a blurred landscape of drizzling sleet without even a trace of robins—a singularly depressing spectacle in mid-May.

At long last my perserverance was rewarded with the sight of a nesting robin—twenty feet up a spruce. With the help of a biologist friend who was endowed with a steadier head for heights, County was again able to thrill to pulsings and movement in the eggs she was warming. The expression in her eyes bore living testimony to her happiness.

Anticipating the demand for bugs soon to come, I installed a child's rigid wading pool in an adjoining room out of the main traffic area, and added a few inches of damp dirt. Then, each day until the hatching, I dropped in small jarfuls of wrigglies, which County hunted enthusiastically—even, to my astonishment, eating the earthworms I'd set in for the babies to come.

At sunrise, a little over a week after the eggs were switched, the even happier look in County's eyes as I passed the nest caused me to stop, climb up on the couch, and look in. She immediately arose and stepped back, revealing a minute pink wriggling baby beneath her. We both gazed at him spellbound. Then County touched him gently with her beak, looked at me, and settled back down over him, her eyes radiant. Spring had come again.

By late afternoon, another little one had hatched and already the difference in size between the two nestlings was very apparent. I stocked the wading pool and County tended the babes, two voices cheeping steadily beneath her during warmings. The following day I watched the third nestling determinedly pushing the eggshell portions apart, with frequent rests. Already the first youngster was twice the size of the newest arrival—a rate of growth that had to be seen to be believed.

ABOUT this time, as I was still keeping a vigilant eye out for mice finding an entrance into the house and thereby inviting weasels, I received a heart-stopping shock. I was outside eyeing the more hopeful progress of the lettuce plants since the warmer weather had arrived, when I heard an outbreak of thumping and knocking coming from inside. Dashing to the window, I peered in anxiously. No birds were visible, although Desmond and Molly should have been right there. I galloped around the corner and bounded into the room to be confronted with wildly-thrashing drapes and the tip of a pigeon's wing protruding. 'Weasels!' was the only clear thought I had as I leapt forward and jerked aside the curtain. A family squabble was revealed. Molly, irate at Desmond for reasons unknown to anyone else, had knocked him down into a crevice between the wall and an old trunk and was systematically and wordlessly pounding him with her wings. Desmond, his own wings jammed tightly and useless, was helplessly enduring her fury.

Poor Desmond. For five thankless years he had faithfully courted Molly, meeting only rebuffs. Perhaps this time, with all the nesting activities indoors and out, he had ventured a tactless comment about feminists. "Hell hath no fury..."

As THE DAYS slipped by, County's little family thrived beautifully, and the overall energy balance was vastly improved. A larger family demanded more output from her, and the wading pool arrangement meant that bugs had to be hunted and dug up before being 'prepared,' an energy outlay that was closer to the natural way. The babies, too, grew at a more natural rate than when only one was being fed—a rate that put less strain on their systems and rendered them less vulnerable to sickness. They kept each other warm, too, while County was foraging. Nevertheless, I took the precaution to analyze their droppings and was relieved to find that all was well.

The new system was an improvement from 'Dad's' point of view too. Provided I had stocked the pool well, unavoidable absences of three or even four hours were possible at this stage—but chancier once the youngsters were out of the nest. By that time, even taking a nap was taking a chance.

The babies grew and grew. County's happiness was so over-flowing that her crest feathers seemed permanently raised in delight. By now the chokecherries were blossoming and I brought in bouquets of them for her to eat, knowing her partiality for them. Even the babes were fed chokecherry blossoms. Earthworms, too, she now ate with gusto, and friends dropping in with gifts of worms were welcomed as warmly by County as by me, her wintertime timidity melting away under her summertime glow of motherhood. The weather turning surprisingly hot, the babes would stretch out their long, thin necks over the rim in three different directions, then sag down with a sigh like three wilted stalks trailing out of the nest, melted and congealed.

In a week all the nestlings were open eyed, beating their wings restlessly and preening tufty feather tips as their quills steadily leafed out, the dark plumage on their heads revealing three young males. They still maintained their nervousness of me, because I was refraining from feeding them in case I had been partially to blame for the illnesses the previous summer. Whenever I did approach to photograph, or just to watch entranced, they often crouched down defensively and soundlessly snapped their beaks, in what I termed their snapping turtle pos-tures. In between active periods they slept deeply, exhausted from growing, while the nest 'shrank' visibly.

Keeping sufficient supplies of bugs and fresh dirt (to counter bacteria buildup) took a goodly portion out of each day. County, as usual, wanted a wide variety. I also noted that she often covered food with dirt or wood ashes before feeding the nestlings—perhaps to aid digestion. No matter what I was eating, she insisted on a taste, and if it seemed suitable, she'd fill her beak with more and carry it off for the family. Fresh steamed and buttered asparagus she adored—fortunately so did they. I drew the line at spicy foods but found it easier to enforce my argument by eating them outside. It was with great mirth that I witnessed her ecstatic delight in ice cream and her futile attempts to transfer dissolving morsels of that savoury concoction up to the nest in the brilliant June heat.

Surrounding us in the wild were numerous other parents also fully occupied each day in finding enough food for their ever hungry broods. So I was unable to feel any annoyance when one blue jay, evidently craftier or bolder than the others, learned about my 'porch trap' for collecting moths and June bugs overnight. Several mornings I startled him out there when I opened the house door, but in none of his frantic ricochets off the screens looking for the exit did he once drop his precious cargo of food. I eventually learned to stagger downstairs and close the outer porch door in the dim pre-dawn dampness, so that something would be still available for County and her babes by the time the light was up. Moths on the outsides of the screens I conceded to the jay, as one sympathetic parent to another.

Less than two weeks after hatching, the firstborn babe was out on the cowhorn and from there, a brief, somewhat dramatic flight dropped him into the garden, the arching plants helpfully cushioning his landing. County was delighted, and the two of them hopped all over the garden and house together, communicating constantly with each other in tiny high sounds, the other nestmates marvelling from the safety of the cowskull. That night, highly independent now, he slept out of the nest, and the following morning found all the babes out and about, with disproportionate long legs and stumpy bottoms. They bounded along eagerly after County, their frumpy bodies nearly as large as their sleek mother's, begging for food in high musical doublenotes and beating their wings excitedly whenever she vigorously 'prepared' wrigglies. Already she was indicating a desire to build her second nest!

The next day I removed the first nest, and brought in fresh materials. That afternoon County was building a second nest. Fortunately for me, she continued to feed the babes, who were learning so quickly that I was astounded the same day to see the youngest actually drinking water. By now, Junebugs were so popular that a gift of about fifty in a jar was devoured in three days, and even the babes themselves began to learn how to pick them up. One advanced learner did very well at pounding a Junebug following County's teaching, but failed to dislodge the stiff wingcases which finally remained sticking out sharply. Swallowing it anyway, his crop, to my awe, swelled out to twice its normal size, and he retired rather thoughtfully to a quiet corner to digest. Another endearing little rascal inside the wading pool was attracted by an escaping worm oozing its determined way up the ramp to the rim above. With admirable tenacity, the youngster floundered repeatedly up the ramp, sliding back down again and again in a tumble of wings and legs, the worm meanwhile departing steadily without a backward glance. Growing up has its difficulties.

Four days after beginning her nest County's first egg came, and an egg a day resulted in a completed clutch of four. She also began 'weaning' the babes during her laying cycle, interweaving occasional feedings with adamant refusals and even trouncing them for emphasis, her staccato insistence ringing out sharply. Two days after her eggs were finished, she woke me at sunrise, thumping down abruptly on my head and barking with earsplitting annoyance, and I knew it was time for the babes to be off. So I gathered them into the porch in order to release them together. I'd witnessed them drinking, bathing, and hunting their own food. Due to my background involvement, they'd never gained trust of humans, so I knew there was nothing else we could teach them. They were ready. Their exuberant confidence outside as they swooped easily through the trees was living proof. As if any further confirmation was needed, County woke me the morning after the release with cozy companionship and soft notes of happiness.

The day after the release, thanks to the same helpful biologist friend, County's four infertile eggs were replaced with three fertile ones, the wild robin still left brooding one. The new ones arrived cunningly kept warm in a bowl lined with cotton batting and sustained carefully with an under-container of water at 40°C. The arrangement worked perfectly. I had distracted County in the wading pool with a fresh shipment of worms while the switch in her nest was made, and when she returned to the eggs, she stood a moment, examining them closely before settling down over them. I was wondering anxiously if she was disturbed by the reduction of her count from four to three. Certainly she would have noticed, not to mention feeling the difference arranging them beneath her, but events the next day indicated that she had also sensed the movements of life inside them. Late that afternoon, when I came downstairs after a much-needed nap, County's eyes were dancing and a tiny voice was cheeping steadily beneath her. Our parenting had begun again.

CHAPTER SIXTEEN

BABIES GALORE

THE SECOND NESTLING HATCHED THE FOLLOWING MORNING; but the third, not until late afternoon of the third day, a gap of about thirty hours, indicating that the third egg laid in the wild robin's clutch must have been the one left with her. County's youngest, therefore, was incredibly smaller than the other two. Although I saw him fed several times, he may have been unable to hold his own with two bigger and more insistent rivals. The day following his hatching, I was obliged to be absent all evening and returned very late. All the birds were bedded down and asleep and I went straight to bed myself.

The next morning I found that County's youngest was dead—a saddening discovery that has troubled me ever since. I removed the tiny body and immediately examined the other two babes, ascertaining that nestling number one was quite strong and vigorous, and that number two was very weak indeed, raising his head with great difficulty. I instantly brought some wrigglies up to the nest, and covered the first babe with my hand so that County would feed the second only. Otherwise, whenever she uttered her 'food cluck,' the energetic firstborn had already been fed and was settling back into the nest by the time the second-born finally raised his head and gaped. So I began supervising every feeding, keeping a special supply of bugs secreted in a covered container solely for the weaker babe, producing them whenever the stronger nestling seemed to be getting more than his share, and constantly comparing the size of their droppings. As a result of this intensive care, the second babe quickly gained strength and size, and after two days was able to thrust his beak up just as quickly as the first. Thereafter all went well, but the whole episode puzzled me exceedingly.

This second time I found County's family life more wearing, not only because of the loss of the littlest one, which led to the ensuing stress of closely monitoring the survivors, but also because of the increasing difficulties of finding enough insect food as the hot, dry weather continued. County, on the other hand, was having a wonderful summer, which was especially gratifying after the frustrations of the previous year. She was truly in her element with all her babies, and her high spirits continually overflowed into our wild games and frolics. With these babes only about twelve days old and not at all inclined to forsake the security of the nest, she not only evinced every desire to build a new nest, she actually got underway, dropping mud and grasses in on top of the inmates and wedging herself in to do the necessary footwork, to their manifest inconvenience. Having experienced the futility of arguing with her, I chose rather to remove the nest, babies and all, and set it on the back of the couch where they passively watched their mother's frenzied flights back and forth from garden to cowskull, with rounded eyes of interest. To me was relegated the task of feeding them every half-hour or so, County being totally engrossed in nest building. Mine, also, was the province of fatigue, County being seemingly immune to it.

The next morning I set the nest with the babies into the wading pool, so that they could at least witness 'Dad' digging up worms—a sort of prep school. Within moments the firstborn was out hopping everywhere, being quickly followed by number two. Before long, they were all over the house while I periodically trailed after them dangling tantalizing worms and chirping beguilingly. Fortunately, their nervousness of me rapidly dissolved with such frequent and welcome bribes of wrigglies, and they gaped readily. Sometimes they returned to sit cozily in the nest again; at night, the younger always slept in it, with the older youngster perched close by. Not all of us mature at the same rate.

County, meanwhile, after beginning on the cowskull, had switched to a different location on a ledge over a door and was progressing quickly. As soon as she was into the final stages of lining the nest with fine material, she began gradually feeding the babes again. I was thankful to be able to devote longer periods of time digging for wrigglies. The first egg came four days after I'd taken the first nest down, and her eyes again resonated that special warmth that spoke of eggs beneath her. Her full clutch was three this time, and as she had completely taken over feeding the fledglings while I retired again to the background, they had begun to feel nervous again toward me, as was necessary. They were the same size as County now, and although their bubbly musical demands for more and more food rarely ceased, I didn't see any signs of them being weaned— none of the trouncings, for instance. They were now about three-and-a-half weeks old, the same age as the first brood when released, and I knew they managed their own feedings when County was on her nest so I decided to release them.

These two babes, however, unlike the first three, were aghast at being loose in the wild and stayed close to the house, calling out shrilly whenever they heard County's voice and landing on the outside of the screen porch to reinforce their protests. They would even answer me each time I called. So in concern, I set out a large flat dish of water, the day being a scorcher, and late in the afternoon I went out and called. With wild welcoming cries, they came swooping through the trees and landed nearby, watching eagerly as I scattered mealworms on the ground and then stepped back. They quickly flew down and tucked in hungrily, obviously not having eaten since they left the house. Although I propped the porch door open till dark, they showed no desire to return inside the house and slept out nearby. But it was evident that these two needed practical assistance adjusting to the wild. The drought, too, rendered the ground hard, dry, and (to my eye) bugless—with my digging abilities, I was experiencing difficulty enough finding wrigglies a foot down. Serviceberries abounded in the trees near the house, but the technique of hovering and seizing these with their beaks they would have to learn from watching other birds. 'Dad,' with all her good intentions had severe limitations, and snapping at hanging berries with her teeth was definitely one of her lesser skills. Nor was I adept at climbing nimbly through dense tree leaves and spotting camouflaged caterpillars. I *could*, however, provide mealworms.

So for the rest of July, I fed both the babes outside, varying the mealworms with nettings of field insects dropped in a twitching mass, and resembling wild food more than the mealworms. Often they bathed simultaneously in the flat waterdish. The older one gradually showed less trust, and returned less and less frequently and for only a week. But the smaller of the two, whom I dubbed 'Little Eyebrows' in honour of his highly-distinctive eyebrows, I fed outside for a total of two weeks. He became a special part of each day's activities, and my thoughts each night hovered anxiously about his unknown roost somewhere in the darkness. We quickly developed quite a rapport—if he caught my eye from one of the windows, he would swoop around to the back door and wait, knowing that I would appear almost immediately with mealworms. If I had to drive off for a couple of hours to take care of errands, or to dig worms elsewhere, invariably Little Eyebrows would be awaiting me on the path when I returned. Often I'd sit out with my tea, and after he'd been fed, he'd remain near me companionably—sometimes trying to provoke sober-minded chipmunks into playing. But their sole interest seemed to be in filling their cheek pouches with bird seed and scuttling back triumphantly to their secret hoards. Another time, I was highly amused watching him jumping and twitching and ruffling his feathers in an ongoing effort to rid himself of something unwanted that was crawling through his plumage.

Gradually I could see that Little Eyebrows was less and less in need of the mealworms, and I tried to feed only supplemental amounts, so that he'd feel hungry enough to persist in hunting his own. Nor did I try to coax him into 'tame' interactions with me, being content to just watch his antics. Once when he picked up a mealworm in the pupa stage, he gave tiny high-pitched squeaks and held it in his beak, giving it deliberate shakes as County would do to feed a babe. He was evidently learning the tricks of survival, drought or no drought; deep blue droppings one day revealed that he'd discovered wild blueberries in the nearby pasture. Another morning I saw both fledglings skillfully pulling off and swallowing serviceberries with the ease of veteran adults. But Little Eyebrows had a charisma of his own, and my natural regret as his inevitable absences lengthened was tempered with satisfaction that he was making his own way at last. Our final connection was hearing him welcome me verbally from the dense tree foliage one day, as I walked up the path to the house. I stopped in delight and peered upward, trying to distinguish his form amid the flickering leaves and shadows. I was being harassed simultaneously by a persistent deerfly, and unthinkingly I swatted it in annoyance. Instantly there rose barks of alarm as a flock of juvenile robins left the trees and Little Eyebrows must have gone with them, responding unquestioningly, as was essential, to the general alarm that indicated danger from a human presence—so much have we lost.

CHAPTER SEVENTEEN

ONE MORE TIME

MEANWHILE, THROUGH THE KIND EFFORTS of a different friend, County had become blessed with two fertile eggs by the time she'd been brooding her own infertile ones at least ten days. She continued to brood another eight or nine days, and then gave up. I was horrified, and strongly remonstrated, but to no avail. The next day, while County undauntedly gathered nesting material for a fourth nest, I took the cold eggs outside and opened them. They had indeed been fertile, but had long since ceased to develop, being in all likelihood dead when she had received them. I had no idea what had happened, but I was relieved to see that County's judgment was as sound as ever.

County returned to the old cowskull site once more, and soon had another beautiful nest in hand and a fourth clutch of three eggs. She again radiated contentment as she warmed and turned them, while I plodded through mile after mile of apparently robin-free wilderness. The topsy-turvy weather was now windy and rainy day after day, and autumn was definitely imminent. I began to have very serious doubts as to whether I could fulfill County's hopes this time. I envisioned her happily brooding and anticipating babies—and plodded on. But the nests were just as elusive as in the early spring days. Wearying finally of the immediate area, I drove ten miles to a friend's home, began combing her area (accompanied by voracious August mosquitoes) and finally was rewarded with a glimpse of, I'm certain, the only nesting robin in the entire province. But the nest, although for once low down in the tree, was at least a half hour's walk through water, across a stubbled hayfield, and up a steep hill before I'd arrive back at my own vehicle—a long haul with a fragile, temperature-sensitive live cargo. The friend came to my rescue with the help of a highly-amused farmer and a rugged half-ton truck good for any terrain. After a long sojourn in the now-relentless sunny weather, waiting till the mother robin left the nest, I quickly approached it and was startled to find two chicks at least three or four days old and two eggs—not likely to hatch. I removed one nestling and, just in case, one egg, leaving the same for the parent upon her return, and sped carefully to the waiting truck where my two accomplices were slowly cooking in the shadeless heat.

We bounced across the field and up the steep rutted road, the farmer very good-naturedly easing the jolts as well as he could and making better speed whenever it was smooth enough to do so, while I tried to keep both babe and egg at a suitable temperature. My tendency was definitely to err on the warm side, and the little one often lay rather alarmingly with his mouth open, regulating his own temperature as birds can do, while we discussed the dire consequences of a welcome breath of cool air. We were all justifiably relieved to arrive at last at the house where I quickly coaxed County off her eggs, removed them and slipped in the new arrivals. Then I coaxed her back to the nest while she looked at me with raised eyebrows. Her astonishment when she finally complied and found herself the mother of a babe whose eyes were already on the verge of opening, only a day after completing her clutch, was delightful and humorous in the extreme. Eyeing the new arrival all over attentively, she touched him two or three times with her beak, prodded the egg as well, gently lowered her brooding feathers and settled snuggily over them both in quiet contentment. The other 'midwives' joined me in rejoicing at our successful venture and finally went their own way, this time, no doubt, with all the windows down. County was a mother again.

'Blimp' grew apace, a rotund nestling seemingly content with being the sole recipient of County's enthusiastic care, and in a couple of days her eyes were open. The egg still not having hatched and showing internal discolouration, I removed it. Blimp's new plumage, meanwhile, steadily leafed out revealing our first daughter of the season. County was delighted with her, and each evening as she warmed her, Blimp would lie gazing up contentedly at County's face and snuggle her head against her while County bent over her, touching her softly, nibbling gently at an unfolding feather, laying her beak against her—enchanting gestures that entranced me. I hadn't noticed any behaviour quite like this before, but then each of County's family experiences was unique.

Blimp's appearance, too, differed again from all the others. To judge by the pale contrasting juvenile feathers around her eyes, her adult eyerings promised to be as large and full as County's. Her beak, too, had a pronounced curve similar to Towne's and Bugs's. And she retained an overall rounder build than any of the previous youngsters even after she was out of the nest—the name truly seemed apt.

Eight days after she'd arrived, Blimp launched herself out of the nest and was active all day. She had been a little congested while she was still nestbound, sneezing frequently and snuffling, although an analysis of her droppings read negative. So I concluded that with the intense humidity, the nest itself might be somewhat musty and irritating to her breathing passages. Once she was out of it, the congestion disappeared and Blimp was on her way. The same day County, to my despair, proceeded to build a fifth nest. How is it that only the fathers get tired in the nesting season?

As she had done previously while building, County left me to feed Blimp—who finally cooperated when she got hungry enough. Thereafter, feedings were easy, and Blimp progressed rapidly, preferring to spend her days in the screened porch rather than the garden. I set a flat dish of water out there with her, and she soon discovered the joys of bathing and sunning. County quickly resumed the feedings once her eggs began coming—her fifth clutch contained three eggs—but quite soon Blimp was picking up bugs on her own and eating chokecherries as well. At this point County began her 'weaning' process, and nearly three weeks after I had brought her home that hot sunny afternoon, Blimp returned to the wild from the porch. As she sat a moment atop the open door, I called her name, and she glanced back at me over her shoulder allowing me one last photograph before departing. Contrary to the release of Little Eyebrows and his brother, Blimp was elated and full of confidence, disdaining subsequent offerings of mealworms and exhibiting complete control of the situation—more after the order of the first brood of the summer. The bug supplies looked more promising outside now, and the chokecherry bushes were laden with fruit. It was an excellent launching.

CHAPTER EIGHTEEN

SATISFACTION

COUNTY BROODED BLISSFULLY, and as I was busily engaged with numerous other concerns which had been piling up alarmingly, she looked for another outlet for her pent-up energies and elected Molly as the victim. Thereafter she teased Molly unmercifully, swooping her, dancing on her head, raiding her waterdish and bathing in it, provoking her however possible—even to the extent of invading Molly's particular house box, an inner sanctum, where she would sit contentedly in the dim interior, cooing softly to herself.

Molly, outraged at these indignities, retaliated vigorously by snatching at and chasing County, even occasionally catching and shaking her despite County's squeals, but this failed to daunt the irrepressible fiend, though she'd be forced to favour a leg or a wing shortly after. Next day, she'd be at it again. If Molly was padding around on the floor, County would deliberately dance around her, keeping just out of range of Molly's snatching beak and leading her from room to room, close enough to tantalize and far enough for her own safety. Then if Molly turned away in disgust, County would leap up, paddle her on the head with her feet, and dart off shrieking derisively while Molly bristled and cooed her annoyance to an empty room. However mellow the late August days may have been outside, with golden fields of light and the soothing hum of crickets, inside there were always fireworks.

THEN one afternoon, about four days after Blimp's release, an adult female robin which had been mauled by a cat was brought to me. She was into her moult, and hopefully had finished raising families when the cat struck. Her chest had been bitten, as well as the right wing and right leg, and her eyes were huge and round with fear and pain. I held her gently in my hands and showed her County watching from the kitchen counter—a reassuring maneuver I had used with other wild birds to calm their fears. Then I put her out into the screened porch with a bunch of chokecherry branches in a jug of water, a small container of drinking water with a drop of tetracycline to combat infection, and a dish of mealworms. I kept the glass door closed into the house so that she'd have privacy from my frightening presence, and also in case any harmful bacteria or parasites could be communicated to County, who was still brooding eggs. In addition, I placed a small stool by the door; County often stopped there, eyeing the new arrival and at first displaying territorially, as was natural.

That first evening as the darkness deepened I feared the worst, for the wild robin, floundering up into the chokecherry branches which were steadied by a twist of driftwood, remained sprawling there, her head hanging down in utter exhaustion. My heart was heavy for her. There was nothing else I could do than to give her a secure place in which to recover or to pass away unmolested by predators. But in the morning when I looked out reluctantly, she was crouched on the table beside the chokecherries in as natural a posture as possible, considering that the toes of her damaged right leg were twisted backward and looked useless. There were also a couple of clean chokecherry pits beside her, which I felt sure were hers. Heartened, I continued to check on her throughout the day and County often perched on the stool or, to the disbelief of our wild guest, on top of my head. 'Peg' steadily progressed.

Her mobility was restricted to 'pegging' awkwardly along on one good foot and the shank end of her bad leg, but she managed. The mealworms, for reasons unknown to me, she shunned till about her third day, but once she'd tasted them, she ate several handfuls daily and her strength returned quickly. Of course, she never lost her fear of me, so I would edge out quietly to replace food and water or to clean the droppings, without looking directly at her, speaking constantly in what I hoped was a soft, soothing tone. Sometimes Peg panicked but often she froze till I had departed. Her enthusiasm for mealworms soon drove her to devouring them before I had quite closed the door, and I'd edge new handfuls out ahead of me whenever her supply needed replenishing so that she'd understand my motives. At these times she usually remained immobile.

In two weeks, the toes on her bad foot were in their natural position, a swelling of a normal colour on the wounded leg betokening scar tissue. The leg still required frequent rests but was definitely returning to normal, her increasing activity providing the necessary therapeutic exercise. Her droppings looked fine and passed analysis, and she cast up chokecherry pits daily so that her internal organs seemed normal. The right wing, which had also been bitten,was definitely not broken but was weak and needed exercise. So I carefully set up another piece of driftwood at the opposite end of the porch from the first. Even that failed to provide enough distance, the porch being only about eight feet long. My presence still filled her with horror, so I hesitated to bring her into the house and thereby increase her stress. But I knew I couldn't keep her in the porch forever, particularly as the entire house roof was due to be reshingled shortly—a project already delayed because of the nesting activities. We were halfway through September too, and I was anxious about Peg's chances to migrate, although there were still lots of robins in the area.

So three weeks after her arrival, I decided to release her. The masses of chokecherry bushes would give her food, and help her to exercise and strengthen the wing. Peg herself was longing to go, and each day sat with her beak pointing south. Weather permitting, robins would be migrating for several weeks yet

As always, I could only hope I'd made the right decision.

AFTER three determined weeks of brooding eggs and harassing Molly, County finally had decided to give up. I had been dreading this moment, since I knew there were no eggs I could have found for her and that even if there had been, the babes would have been released well into September, which was very late for youngsters. If such babies did exist in the wild, I preferred that they should be with their parents—a sensible precaution. As well, I would never have managed to provide the necessary insect food—my foraging for Blimp had produced desperately small quantities even after hours of digging.

So I had worried about County's inevitable disappointment. For two days she sat moodily in retired corners, uttering plaintive high notes of intense feeling, while I talked comfortingly to her and plied her with a variety of tasty tidbits. She also slept on the empty nest, although I had clandestinely removed the eggs. Then suddenly one night she began 'migrating,' and her depression, to my great relief, completely vanished. She was active day and night, and the rooms resounded once again with her piercing migration whistles. Her high spirits became the norm, her eyes glowed with happiness, and her crest feathers positively stood on end. She again became my shadow, sleeping part of each night on my head, calling after me if I left the room, and generally staying near, her eyes full of smiles.

All was well. The lessons I had learned the previous summer and the resolves I had undertaken, had borne fruit in a wonderfully-balanced nesting season for one very special robin who now had the feeling of fulfillment to carry her through the winter. And I had an enriching wealth of insight and experience to muse upon and digest—only possible from knowing County.

Epilogue

FOLLOWING HER MIGRATION that last fall, County astonished me yet again by building a sixth nest and laying three more eggs, which she brooded for three weeks—until mid-November. Then she abruptly began to moult, dropping enormous quantities of feathers in only a few days which rendered her unable to fly. Her activities were restricted to continual preening on the drying pegs over the woodstove, and I set up a 'ladder' of stools and boards so that she could regain her warm perch on the difficult occasions when she fell off. I also set food and water beside her, since it was too awkward for her to come down for them. By December, she had finally regained her accustomed beautiful plumage and was full of playfulness and song—even catching flies and crickets with her usual dexterity. She continued to roost each evening on the pegs over the stove which was in the living room.

One day, in mid-December, I came home after dark, expecting County to be asleep in the living room, as usual. But as I struggled through the door into the darkened porch, overladen with several bags of groceries, County, roosting instead just inside the porch, was suddenly startled by my noisy entrance and shot instantly towards the only available brightness—the outside light. In a split-second she was high up in a spruce tree in complete darkness. My utmost efforts all through the night and the next few days failed to locate her. I never saw her again.

THAT same endless night, as I sat by the wood stove and made numerous trips outside into the bitter darkness to call her, I was given a sudden vision of her. For a moment, she stood looking at me in radiant happiness, her eyerings glowing golden, her 'smile' directed towards me, and I knew that I was seeing County beyond this Threshold. Her happiness looked greater than it ever had here, and I was grateful for the comfort that managed to pierce my desolation.